Advances in Quasi-Experimental Design and Analysis

William M. K. Trochim, *Editor*
Cornell University

NEW DIRECTIONS FOR PROGRAM EVALUATION
A Publication of the American Evaluation Association
*A joint organization of the Evaluation Research Society
and the Evaluation Network*
MARK W. LIPSEY, *Editor-in-Chief*
Claremont Graduate School

Number 31, Fall 1986

Paperback sourcebooks in
The Jossey-Bass Higher Education and
Social and Behavioral Sciences Series

Jossey-Bass Inc., Publishers
San Francisco • London

William M. K. Trochim (ed.).
Advances in Quasi-Experimental Design and Analysis.
New Directions for Program Evaluation, no. 31.
San Francisco: Jossey-Bass, 1986.

New Directions for Program Evaluation Series
A Publication of the American Evaluation Association
Mark W. Lipsey, *Editor-in-Chief*

New Directions for Program Evaluation (publication number USPS
449-050) is published quarterly by Jossey-Bass Inc., Publishers, and is
sponsored by the American Evaluation Association. Second-class
postage paid at San Francisco, California, and at additional
mailing offices. POSTMASTER: Send address change to
Jossey-Bass Inc., Publishers, 433 California Street,
San Francisco, California 94104.

Editorial correspondence should be sent to the Editor-in-Chief,
Mark Lipsey, Psychology Department, Claremont Graduate School,
Claremont, Calif. 91711.

Library of Congress Catalog Number 85-81899

International Standard Serial Number ISSN 0164-7989

International Standard Book Number 1-55542-990-4

Cover art by WILLI BAUM

Manufactured in the United States of America

Ordering Information

The paperback sourcebooks listed below are published quarterly and can be ordered either by subscription or single-copy.

Subscriptions cost $40.00 per year for institutions, agencies, and libraries. Individuals can subscribe at the special rate of $30.00 per year *if payment is by personal check.* (Note that the full rate of $40.00 applies if payment is by institutional check, even if the subscription is designated for an individual.) Standing orders are accepted.

Single copies are available at $9.95 when payment accompanies order, and *all single-copy orders under $25.00 must include payment.* (California, New Jersey, New York, and Washington, D.C., residents please include appropraite sales tax.) For billed orders, cost per copy is $9.95 plus postage and handling. (Prices subject to change without notice.)

Bulk orders (ten or more copies) of any individual sourcebook are available at the following discounted prices: 10–49 copies, $8.95 each; 50–100 copies, $7.96 each; over 100 copies, *inquire.* Sales tax and postage and handling charges apply as for single copy orders.

Please note that these prices are for the academic year 1986–1987 and are subject to change without prior notice. Also, some titles may be out of print and therefore not available for sale.

To ensure correct and prompt delivery, all orders must give either the *name of an individual* or an *official purchase order number.* Please submit your order as follows:

Subscriptions: specify series and year subscription is to begin.
Single-Copies: specify sourcebook code (such as, PE1) and first two words of title.

Mail orders for United States and Possessions, Latin America, Canada, Japan, Australia, and New Zealand to:
> Jossey-Bass Inc., Publishers
> 433 California Street
> San Francisco, California 94104

Mail orders for all other parts of the world to:
> Jossey-Bass Limited
> 28 Banner Street
> London ECIY 8QE

New Directions for Program Evaluation
Mark W. Lipsey, *Editor-in-Chief*

Contents

New Directions for Program Evaluation

A Quarterly Publication of the American Evaluation Association
(A Joint Organization of the Evaluation Research Society and
Evaluation Network)

Editor-in-Chief:

Mark W. Lipsey, Psychology, Claremont Graduate School

Editorial Advisory Board:

Scarvia B. Andersen, Psychology, Georgia Institute of Technology
Gerald L. Barkdoll, U.S. Food and Drug Administration, Washington D.C.
Robert F. Boruch, Psychology, Northwestern University
Timothy C. Brock, Psychology, Ohio State University
Donald T. Campbell, Social Relations, Lehigh University
Eleanor Chelimsky, U.S. General Accounting Office, Washington D.C.
James A. Ciarlo, Mental Health Systems Evaluation, University of Denver
Ross F. Conner, Social Ecology, University of California, Irvine
William W. Cooley, Learning, Research, and Development Center, University
   of Pittsburgh
David S. Cordray, Psychology, Northwestern University
Robert W. Covert, Evaluation Research Center, University of Virginia
Lois-ellin Datta, U.S. General Accounting Office, Washington D.C.
Barbara Gross Davis, Educational Development, University of California,
   Berkeley
Howard E. Freeman, Sociology, University of California, Los Angeles
Egon G. Guba, Education, Indiana University
Edward S. Halpern, AT&T Bell Laboratories, Naperville, Illinois
Harry P. Hatry, The Urban Institute, Washington D.C.
Michael Hendricks, MH Associates, Washington D.C.
Gary T. Henry, Joint Legislative Audit and Review Commission, Virginia
Dennis H. Holmes, Education, George Washington University
Ernest R. House, CIRCE, University of Illinois, Urbana-Champaign
Jeanette M. Jerrell, Cognos Associates, Los Altos, California
Karen E. Kirkhart, Educational Psychology, University of Texas, Austin
Henry M. Levin, Education, Stanford University
Richard J. Light, Government, Harvard University
Charles McClintock, Human Service Studies, Cornell University
William A. McConnell, San Francisco Community Mental Health Programs
Jeri Nowakowski, Leadership & Educ. Policy Studies, Northern Illinois
   University
Michael Q. Patton, International Programs, University of Minnesota

American Evaluation Association, 9555 Persimmon Tree Road, Potomac, MD 20854

Editor's Notes

The intent of this volume is to update, perhaps even to alter, our thinking about quasi-experimentation in applied social research and program evaluation. Since Campbell and Stanley (1963) introduced the term *quasi-experiment,* we have tended to see this area as involving primarily two interrelated topics: the theory of the validity of casual inferences and a taxonomy of the research designs that enable us to examine causal hypotheses. We can see this in the leading expositions of quasi-experimentation (Campbell and Stanley, 1963, 1966; Cook and Campbell, 1979) as well as in the standard textbook presentations of the topic (Kidder and Judd, 1986; Rossi and Freeman, 1985), where it is typical to have separate sections or chapters that discuss validity issues first and then proceed to distinguishable quasi-experimental designs (for example, the pretest-posttest nonequivalent group design, the regression-discontinuity design, the interrupted time series design). My first inclination in editing this volume was to emulate this tradition, beginning the volume with a chapter on validity and following it with a chapter for each of the major quasi-experimental designs that raised the relevant conceptual and analytical issues and discussed recent advances. But, I think, such an approach would have simply contributed to a persistent confusion about the nature of quasi-experimentation and its role in research.

Instead, this volume makes the case that we have moved beyond the traditional thinking on quasi-experiments as a collection of specific designs and threats to validity toward a more integrated, synthetic view of quasi-experimentation as part of a general logical and epistemological framework for research. To support this view that the notion of quasi-experimentation is evolving toward increasing integration, I will discuss a number of themes that seem to characterize our current thinking and that cut across validity typologies and design taxonomies. This list of themes may also be viewed as a tentative description of the advances in our thinking about quasi-experimentation in social research.

The Role of Judgment

One theme that underlies most of the others and that illustrates our increasing awareness of the tentativeness and frailty of quasi-experimentation concerns the importance of human judgment in research. Evidence

I wish to thank Bonnie Sterling for her patience and assistance in the preparation of this volume.

bearing on a causal relationship can emerge from many sources, and it is not a trivial matter to integrate or resolve conflicts or discrepancies. In recognition of this problem of evidence, we are beginning to address causal inference as a psychologcal issue that can be illuminated by cognitive models of the judgmental process (see Chapter One of this volume and Einhorn and Hogarth, 1986). We are also recognizing more clearly the sociological bases of scientific thought (Campbell, 1984) and the fact that science is at root a human enterprise. Thus, a positivist, mechanistic view is all but gone from quasi-experimental thinking, and what remains is a more judgmental and more scientifically sensible perspective.

The Case for Tailored Designs

Early expositions of quasi-experimentation took a largely taxonomic approach, laying out a collection of relatively discrete research designs and discussing how weak or strong they were for valid causal inference. Almost certainly, early proponents recognized that there was a virtual infinity of design variations and that validity was more complexly related to theory and context than their presentations implied. Nonetheless, what seemed to evolve was a "cookbook" approach to quasi-experimentation that involved "choosing" a design that fit the situation and checking off lists of validity threats.

In an important paper on the coupling of randomized and nonrandomized design features, Boruch (1975) explicitly encouraged us to construct research designs as combinations of more elemental units (for example, assignment strategies, measurement occasions) based on the specific contextual needs and plausible alternative explanations for a treatment effect. This move toward hybrid, tailored, or patched-up designs, which involved suggesting how such designs could be accomplished, is one in which I have been a minor participant (Trochim and Land, 1982; Trochim, 1984). It is emphasized by Cordray in Chapter One of this volume. The implication for current practice is that we should focus on the advantages of different combinations of design features rather than on a relatively restricted set of prefabricated designs. In teaching quasi-experimental methods, we need to break away from a taxonomic design mentality and emphasize design principles and issues that cut across the traditional distinctions between true experiments, nonexperiments, and quasi-experiments.

The Crucial Role of Theory

Quasi-experimentation and its randomized experimental parent have been criticized for encouraging an atheoretical "black box" mentality of research (see, for instance, Chen and Rossi, 1984; Cronbach, 1982). Persons are assigned to either complex molar program packages or (often) to equally complex comparison conditions. The machinery of random assignment (or our quasi-experimental attempts to approximate random assignment) are the primary means of defining whether the program has an effect. This ceteris paribus mentality is inherently atheoretical and noncontextual: It assumes that the same mechanism works in basically the same way whether we apply it in mental health or criminal justice, income maintenance or education.

There is nothing inherently wrong with this program-group-versus-comparison-group logic. The problem is that it may be a rather crude, uninformative approach. In the two-group case, we are simply creating a dichotomous input into reality. If we observe a posttest difference between groups, it could be explained by this dichotomous program-versus-comparison-group input or by any number of alternative explanations, including differential attrition rates, intergroup rivalry and communication, initial selection differences among groups, or different group histories. We usually try to deal with these alternative explanations by ruling them out through argument, additional measurement, patched-up design features, and auxiliary analysis. Cook and Campbell (1979), Cronbach (1982), and others strongly favor replication of treatment effects as a standard for judging the validity of a causal assertion, but this advice does little to enhance the validity and informativeness within individual studies or program evaluations.

Chen and Rossi (1984, p. 339) approached this issue by advocating increased attention to social science theory: "not the global conceptual schemes of the grand theorists but much more prosaic theories that are concerned with how human organizations work and how social problems are generated." Evaluators have similarly begun to stress the importance of program theory as the basis for causal assessment (for example, Bickman, in press). These developments allow increased emphasis to be placed on the role of pattern matching (Trochim, 1985) through the generation of more complex theory-driven predictions that, if corroborated, allow fewer plausible alternative explanations for the effect of a program. Because appropriate theories may not be readily available, especially for the evaluation of contemporary social programs, we are developing methods and processes that facilitate the articulation of the implicit theories which program administrators and stakeholder groups have in mind and which presumably guide the formation and implementation of the program (Trochim, 1985). This theory-driven perspective is consonant with Mark's emphasis in Chapter Three on the study of causal process and with Cordray's discussion in Chapter One on ruling in the program as opposed to ruling out alternative explanations.

Attention to Program Implementation

A theory-driven approach to quasi-experimentation will be futile unless we can demonstrate that the program was in fact carried out or implemented as the theory intended. Consequently, we have seen the development of program implementation theory (for example, McLaughlin, 1984) that directly addresses the process of program execution. One approach emphasizes the development of organizational procedures and training systems that accurately transmit the program and that anticipate likely institutional sources of resistance. Another strategy involves the assessment of program delivery through program audits, management information systems, and the like. This emphasis on program implementation has further obscured the traditional distinction between process and outcome evaluation. At the least, it is certainly clear that good quasi-experimental outcome evaluation cannot be accomplished without attending to program processes, and we are continuing to develop better notions of how to combine these two efforts.

The Importance of Quality Control

Over and over, our experience with quasi-experimentation has shown that even the best-laid research plans often go awry in practice, sometimes with disastrous results. Thus, over the past decade we have begun to pay increasing attention to the integrity and quality of our research methods in real-world settings. One way of achieving this goal is to incorporate techniques used by other professions—accounting, auditing, industrial quality control—that have traditions in data integrity and quality assurance (Trochim and Visco, 1985). For instance, double bookkeeping can be used to keep verifiable records of research participation. Acceptance sampling can be an efficient method for checking accuracy in large data collection efforts, where an exhaustive examination of records is impractical or excessive in cost. These issues are particularly important in quasi-experimentation, where it is incumbent upon the researcher to demonstrate that sampling, measurement, group assignment, and analysis decisions do not interact with program participation in ways that can confound the final interpretation of results.

The Advantages of Multiple Perspectives

We have long recognized the importance of replication and systematic variation in research. In the past few years, Cook (1985) and colleagues Shadish and Houts (Chapter Two in this volume) have articulated a rationale for achieving systematic variation that they term *critical multiplism*. This perspective rests on the notion that no single realization will ever be sufficient for understanding a phenomenon with validity. Multiple realizations—of research questions, measures, samples, designs, analyses, replications, and so on—are essential for convergence on the truth of a matter. However, such a varied approach can become a methodological and epistemological

Pandora's box unless we apply critical judgment in deciding which multiples we will emphasize in a study or set of studies (Chapter Two in this volume and Mark and Shotland, 1985).

Evolution of the Concept of Validity

The history of quasi-experimentation is inseparable from the development of the theory of the validity of causal inference. Much of this history has been played out through the ongoing dialogue between Campbell and Cronbach concerning the definition of validity and the relative importance that should be attributed on the one hand to the establishment of a causal relationship and on the other hand to its generalizability. In the most recent major statement in this area, Cronbach (1982) articulated the UTOS model, which conceptually links the units, treatments, observing operations and settings in a study into a framework that can be used for establishing valid causal inference. The dialogue continues in Chapter Four of this volume, where Campbell attempts to dispel persistent confusion about the types of validity by tentatively relabeling *internal validity* as *local molar causal validity* and *external validity* as the *principle of proximal similarity*. It is reasonable to hope that we might achieve a clearer consensus on this issue, as Mark argues in Chapter Three, where he attempts to resolve several different conceptions of validity, including those of Campbell and Cronbach.

Development of Increasingly Complex Realistic Analytic Models

In the past decade, we have made considerable progress toward complicating our statistical analyses to account for increasingly complex contexts and designs. One such advance involves the articulation of causal models of the sort described by Reichardt and Gollob in Chapter Six, especially models that allow for latent variables and that directly model measurement error (Jöreskog and Sörbom, 1979).

Another important recent development involves analyses that address the problem of selection bias or group nonequivalence—a central issue in quasi-experiments because random assignment is not used and there is no assurance that comparison groups are initially equivalent (Rindskopf's discussion in Chapter Five). At the same time, there is increasing recognition of the implications of not attending to the correct unit of analysis when analyzing the data and of the advantages and implications of conducting analyses at multiple levels. Thus, when we assign classrooms to conditions but analyze individual student data rather than classroom aggregates, we are liable to get a different view of program effects than we are when we analyze at the classroom level, as Shadish, Cook, and Houts argue in Chapter Two. Other notable advances that are not explicitly addressed in this volume include the development of log linear, probit, and logit models for the analysis of qualitative or nominal level outcome variables (Feinberg, 1980; Forthofer and Lehnen, 1981) and the increasing proliferation of Bayesian statistical approaches to quasi-experimental contexts (Pollard, 1986).

Parallel to the development of these increasingly complex, realistic analytic models, cynicism has deepened about the ability of any single model or analysis to be sufficient. Thus, in Chapter Six Reichardt and Gollob call for multiple analyses to bracket bias, and in Chapter Five Rindskopf recognizes the assumptive notions of any analytic approach to selection bias. We have virtually abandoned the hope of a single correct analysis, and we have accordingly moved to multiple analyses that are based on systematically distinct assumptional frameworks and that rely in an increasingly direct way on the role of judgment.

Conclusion

All the developments just outlined point to an increasingly realistic and complicated life for quasi-experimentalists. The overall picture that emerges is that all quasi-experimentation is judgmental. It is based on multiple and varied sources of evidence, it should be multiplistic in realization, it must attend to process as well as to outcome, it is better off when theory driven, and it leads ultimately to multiple analyses that attempt to bracket the program effect within some reasonable range.

In one sense, this is hardly a pretty picture. Our views about quasi-experimentation and its role in causal inference are certainly more tentative and critical than they were in 1965 or perhaps even in 1979. But, this more integrated and complex view of quasi-experimentation has emerged directly from our experiences in the conduct of such studies. As such, it realistically represents our current thinking about one of the major strands in the evolution of social research methodology in this century.

William M. K. Trochim.
Editor

References

Bickman, L. (ed.). *Program Theory and Program Evaluation*. New Directions for Program Evaluation, no. 33. San Francisco: Jossey-Bass, in press.

Boruch, R. F. "Coupling Randomized Experiments and Approximations to Experiments in Social Program Evaluation." *Sociological Methods and Research*, 1975, *4* (1), 31–53.

Campbell, D. T. "Can We Be Scientific in Applied Social Science?" In R. F. Conner and others (eds.), *Evaluation Studies Review Annual*. Vol. 9. Beverly Hills, Calif.: Sage, 1984.

Campbell, D. T., and Stanley, J. C. "Experimental and Quasi-Experimental Designs for Research on Teaching." In N. L. Gage (ed.), *Handbook of Research on Teaching.* Chicago: Rand McNally, 1963.

Campbell, D. T., and Stanley, J. C. *Experimental and Quasi-Experimental Designs for Research.* Chicago: Rand McNally, 1966.

Chen, H., and Rossi, P. A. "Evaluating with Sense: The Theory-Driven Approach." In R. F. Conner and others (eds.), *Evaluation Studies Review Annual.* Vol. 9. Beverly Hills, Calif.: Sage, 1985.

Cook, T. D. "Postpositivist Critical Multiplism." In R. L. Shotland and M. M. Mark (eds.), *Social Science and Social Policy.* Beverly Hills, Calif.: Sage, 1985.

Cook, T. D., and Campbell, D. T. *Quasi-Experimentation: Design and Analysis Issues for Field Settings.* Chicago: Rand McNally, 1979.

Cronbach, L. J. *Designing Evaluations of Educational and Social Programs.* San Francisco: Jossey-Bass, 1982.

Einhorn, H. J., and Hogarth, R. M. "Judging Probable Cause." *Psychologcal Bulletin,* 1986 *99,* 3–19.

Feinberg, S. E. *The Analysis of Cross-Classified Categorical Data.* (2nd ed.) Cambridge, Mass.: M.I.T. Press, 1980.

Forthofer, R. N., and Lehnen, R. G. *Public Program Analysis: A New Categorical Data Approach.* Belmont, Calif.: Wadsworth, 1981.

Jöreskog, K. G., and Sörbom, D. *Advances in Factor Analysis and Structural Equation Models.* Cambridge: Abt Books, 1979.

Kidder, L. H., and Judd, C. M. *Research Methods in Social Relations.* (5th ed.) New York: Holt, Rinehart & Winston, 1986.

Mark, M. M., and Shotland, R. L. "Toward More Useful Social Science." In R. L. Shotland and M. M. Mark (eds.), *Social Science and Social Policy.* Beverly Hills, Calif.: Sage, 1985.

McLaughlin, M. W. "Implementation Realities and Evaluation Design." In R. L. Shotland and M. M. Mark (eds.), *Social Science and Social Policy.* Beverly Hills, Calif.: Sage, 1984.

Pollard, W. E. *Bayesian Statistics for Evaluation Research.* Beverly Hills, Calif.: Sage, 1986.

Rossi, P. H., and Freeman, H. E. *Evaluation: A Systematic Approach.* (3rd ed.) Beverly Hills, Calif.: Sage, 1985.

Trochim, W. *Research Design for Program Evaluation: The Regression-Discontinuity Approach.* Beverly Hills, Calif.: Sage, 1984.

Trochim, W. "Pattern Matching, Validity, and Conceptualization in Program Evaluation." *Evaluation Review,* 1985, *9* (5), 575–604.

Trochim, W., and Land, D. "Designing Designs for Research." *The Researcher,* 1982, *1* (1), 1–6.

Trochim, W., and Visco, R. "Quality Control in Evaluation." In D. S. Cordray (ed.), *Utilizing Prior Research in Evaluation Planning.* New Directions for Program Evaluation, no. 27. San Francisco: Jossey-Bass, 1985.

William M. K. Trochim is assistant professor in the Department of Human Service Studies in the College of Human Ecology at Cornell University. He is author of a book on quasi-experimental research design entitled Research Design for Program Evaluation: The Regression-Discontinuity Approach. *He has written on a wide range of topics related to program evaluation, including experimental and quasi-experimental research, statistical analyses for selection bias, program implementation, research quality control, statistical simulation, and conceptualization methods.*

The role of human judgment in the development and synthesis of evidence has not been adequately developed or acknowledged within quasi-experimental analysis. Like ordinary causal inference, comprehensive causal analysis requires not only consideration of plausible rival explanations but evidence that the purported causal agent is itself plausible.

Quasi-Experimental Analysis: A Mixture of Methods and Judgment

David S. Cordray

The recent technical and conceptual literature on quasi-experimental analysis reveals several major advances. Methods of statistical analysis have become increasingly sophisticated, allowing us to estimate parameters in complex causal models. Moreover, due to improved diagnostic tests, our ability to determine if (and how well) data fit these models has also been greatly enhanced. Further, to counter the other imperfections in quasi-experimental analysis of causal relations, the use of multiple strategies (for example, methods, measures, analysts) has been widely advocated.

Despite this continuous parade of advances, evaluations following the quasi-experimental paradigm continue to exhibit serious flaws. While it is reasonable to expect that some fraction of studies will be inadequate, the literature appears to contain a disproportionate number of poor studies. For example, the U.S. General Accounting Office (1984) conducted an evaluation synthesis of studies purporting to assess the impact of the Women, Infants, and Children (WIC) program. Of the sixty-one studies reviewed, only six were sufficiently relevant, credible, and well reported to be used to examine the effects of WIC on birthweight of infants.

Unfortunately, such weaknesses are not isolated in particular substantive areas (Gilbert and others, 1975; Lipsey and others, 1985). They have been reported in assessments of evaluations of youth employment training

W. M. K. Trochim (ed.). *Advances in Quasi-Experimental Design and Analysis.*
New Directions for Program Evaluation, no. 31. San Francisco: Jossey-Bass, Fall 1986.

9

programs (Betsey and others, 1985), juvenile justice (Maltz and others, 1980; Wright and Dixon, 1977), education (Boruch and Cordray, 1980), maternal and child health (Shadish and Reis, 1984), and in medical trials (Chalmers, 1982). The relatively high incidence of technically poor studies is not a trivial problem; it poses a serious threat to the reputation of the field.

What factors have contributed to this state of affairs? Many reasons have been offered. Some programs may not have been well enough developed for meaningful experimentation. Studies included in the reviews may have been planned and conducted long before sophisticated technology was available. A less hopeful interpretation is that we may be expecting too much of social science methods, that is, they may be inherently too crude to match the complexity of social programs. A still less generous reason might also be offered: As a profession, we simply may not have learned when and how to conduct these assessments properly. As a way of accounting for the relatively poor showing of prior quasi-experimental evaluations, each of these reasons probably contributes some understanding of the problem, and each implies a different set of solutions.

Rather than focusing on statistical issues or conceptual frameworks as corrective mechanisms, this chapter examines the role of judgment within quasi-experimentation. The next section examines the conventional criteria for establishing causal relations, shows how they are too simplistic for quasi-experimental anlysis, and draws on principles derived from the psychology of judging causality as a way of broadening the evidence needed for causal analyses. On the basis of this broad framework, two forms of quasi-experimental analysis are then reviewed: structural models and "patched-up" analyses. The development of a broad evidential base and the synthesis of evidence are described for each form. The pattern of strengths and weaknesses for each approach reveals that improvements in quasi-experimentation require attention both to issues in research methodology and to human judgment.

What Is Missing in Quasi-Experimentation?

A review of the empirical literature seems to indicate that the role of judgment within quasi-experimentation has neither been fully acknowledged nor properly employed in practice. Herein lies one of the fundamental problems in quasi-experimental analysis.

The Criteria for Causal Relations Are Impoverished. Within the logic of evidence used for testing cause-effect relationships, it is generally believed that causal relationships are established if three conditions hold: First, the purported cause (X) precedes the effect (Y); second, X covaries with Y; third, all other rival explanations are implausible. In the ideal case, if these conditions are met, they allow us to state a "fact" (for example, the treatment caused an increase in performance), with the separate effects of "artifacts" held in check. The third condition plays an especially important role in causal inference. The credibility (or strength) of the evidence about a causal claim is greatest when no plausible alternative explanation can be invoked, and it is lower when such alternatives are available. Causal inferences derived from quasi-experimental analyses rarely satisfy this condition; that is, the internal validity of the inference is always suspect.

If the most distinctive feature of causal analysis is the need to discount the influence of other factors, our view of causal evidence is inherently limited. Einhorn and Hogarth (1986) liken the diagnostic value of discounting other explanations to the case of the mystery writer who only reveals who did *not* commit the crime. Similarly, covariation of cause and effect is too simplistic a criterion when X is part of a complex set of factors that influence Y. And, while X must occur before Y occurs, temporal contiguity is low or ambiguous in many field applications. Thus, while the classic criteria for establishing causal relationships may be adequate guides for the development of evidence in relatively closed systems, a more comprehensive set of guiding principles is needed for quasi-experimental analysis in open systems like program research.

The Role of Methodology and Judgment. If we grant that the criteria for establishing causal relationships are impoverished, the question then becomes, On what grounds can we derive a more comprehensive notion of evidence within quasi-experimental assessment? One way of approaching this question is by looking at the judgmental tasks that an analyst must perform. In practice, quasi-experimental analysis falls somewhere between pure reliance on scientific methods and pure human judgment. A reasonable set of principles on evidence within quasi-experimentation must take this mixture of methodology and judgment into account. In particular, issues about evidence appear in two distinct tasks: the development of a data acquisition plan and the synthesis or combination of evidence into a coherent set of results. In both tasks, the analyst exerts considerable discretion over the evidence to include, its completeness and relevance, and how it should be combined and presented in making a summary judgment about the strength of the causal relationship. Often, the analyst is required to derive conclusions about the effects of an intervention by piecing together numerous bits of information accumulated by multiple methods—a process akin to Sherlock Holmes's investigative tactics (Larson and Kaplan, 1981; Leamer, 1978). Since many issues implied by these practices fall outside the domain of classical statistical theory, the literature has been largely mute regarding solutions to these combinatorial procedures. Those who have begun to grapple with these issues (Finney, 1974; Fennessey, 1976; Gilbert and others, 1976; Leamer, 1978) identify many problems faced by users of multimethod strategies, for example, nonindependence of evidence and the resulting overconfidence in conclusions, judgments about the differential credibility of evidence, and data-instigated specification searches. The questions then become, How can complex and diverse sources of evidence be combined to form an overall judgment of the strength of a causal relationship? and, Are some intuitively appealing procedures subject to inferential difficulties? The answers to these questions depend on the types of methodologies that are employed and on the degree to which human judgment is involved.

As such, it seems useful to begin by examining the systematic rules that people use in judging ordinary causal relations. This perspective has two benefits. First, since judgment plays a central role in quasi-experimental analysis, an examination of the evidence on stereotypical biases or flaws that individuals exhibit can lead to corrective solutions on the development and synthesis tasks. Second, the results of an analysis in applied research are often intended to be used by others, such as policy makers. Gaining an understanding of the way in which causal evidence is interpreted can also help to ensure that the evidence that is developed is maximally credible and useful.

Features of Ordinary Causal Judgments. Einhorn and Hogarth's (1986) review of the literature on judging probable cause asserts that scientific and ordinary causal inference are made both within the context of a causal field and in light of interrelationships among several cues-to-causality (that is, temporal order, distinctiveness, strength of the causal chain, covariation, congruity, and contiguity). When these factors are combined, they determine the perception of the overall gross strength of the causal relation. The Einhorn and Hogarth formulation of the psychology of judging probable cause has several implications for the ways in which we conduct and disclose our formal causal assessments of the effects of interventions. First, the relevance of a particular causal explanation (the treatment or a rival explanation) depends critically on its role within a causal field, that is, on a specified set of contextual factors. The causal field sets the context for interpretation of differences among variables and deviations from expectations or steady states, and it limits or expands the number and salience of alternative explanations. For a cause to be plausible, its distinctiveness from the background must be considered within the particular causal field. For program research, this means that the strength and fidelity of the treatment (relative to no-treatment conditions) must be determined. This is rarely done in practice (Scheirer and Rezmovic, 1983).

Second, in contrast to the conventional notion of covariation, Einhorn and Hogarth's formulation suggests that covariation need not be perfect in order to instigate a causal inference. More important, when people judge that X caused Y, "they rarely mean that X is either necessary or sufficient for Y" (Einhorn and Hogarth, 1986, p. 7). Rather, X is seen as conjoined with a particular set of conditions as part of a complex scenario; this is all couched within a specified causal field (B). Einhorn and Hogarth express this complex scenario as $\propto = (X \cap W \cap Z \mid B)$, where X is a necessary but insufficient part of the complex scenario that is itself unnecessary but sufficient to produce Y. This means that other causes of Y exist, and only a specific set of conditions conjoins with X to produce Y in a given causal field. What these conditions are in practice depends on the program model, theory, and particulars of the setting.

Third, the Einhorn and Hogarth model differs from the classical criteria in its explicit recognition of the need to establish causal chains to account for overall strength of the relationship. Within this notion are two interdependent factors, contiguity and congruity. Contiguity refers to the extent to which events are contiguous in time and space. When contiguity is low (for example, when substantial time elapses between the presence of X and the appearance of Y), a causal relation is difficult to justify unless intermediate causal models are established to link the events. Congruity refers to the similarity of the strength (or duration) of cause and effect. In its simplest form, the notion of congruity implies that strong causes produce strong effects and that weak causes produce weak effects. This, of course, is too simple. To account for seemingly anomalous relations (for example, small causes that produce big effects), additional processes must be specified that justify how the cause must have been amplified (large effect, given a small cause) or dampened (small effect, given a large cause) so as to produce the observed magnitude of effect.

Taken together, contiguity and congruity form the basis for specifying the length of the causal chain necessary to link X with Y. When both are high, few if any links are needed. When congruity is low and contiguity is high, the mechanisms that dampen or amplify the effect must be considered; similarly, in the reverse case, links that bridge the contiguity gap are necessary. The most complex case is that in which both contiguity and congruity are low. Here, intermediate causal links are needed both to bridge the temporal gap and to represent the amplification or dampening process.

What Does This Imply for Quasi-Experimental Analysis?

The psychology of judging probable cause makes it clear that the types of evidence that are brought to bear in causal analysis cannot be limited to the simplistic input-output conception implied by the three classic cues-to-causality discussed earlier. This is particularly true for quasi-experimental analysis, which usually does not rule out all rival explanatons. To the extent to which policy makers can muster their own rival explanations or the findings are uncertain, the credibility of the results can be questioned, or—worse—the findings can be disregarded entirely. For example, in the absence of sufficient detail on the change process, it becomes legitimate to ask, How did a puny treatment, installed in a "noisy" environment, cause a harmful effect on performance? One obvious answer—right or wrong—is that there must be something wrong with the methods used to derive the inference. Indeed, if a plausible model cannot be postulated, this seems a reasonable answer.

Credibility of Evidence. Einhorn and Hogarth's (1986) review of the literature on judging probable cause is concerned with the phenomenology of causal inference, that is, with the perception of causality. It is not necessary to specify whether the individual has correctly identified the true causal relationships. Quasi-experimentation is somewhat more structured than this in the sense that rules of evidence have been established for determining the credibility of evidence under various design configurations. As such, we need to add a second feature to the psychology of judging causal relations, namely judgments about the probative value of the evidence. An analogous consideration within jurisprudence has been highlighted by Schum and Martin (1982). For instance a witness may state a fact (for example, the defendant was at the scene of the crime). Before the inference that the defendant committed the crime can be made, the credibility of the witness must be considered. In program research terms, suppose that an analysis shows no treatment effect. Before we can infer that the treatment did not work, we must have evidence that the treatment (that is, the cause) was indeed present and that the methodology was sensitive enough to detect any effect that it may have produced.

Three General Considerations. The notion of evidence within quasi-experimental analysis needs to be extended beyond the prevalent cues-to-causality established within the classic experimental paradigm. The preceding discussion on the psychology of judging probable cause suggests that a comprehensive view of evidence within quasi-experimental analysis requires at least three additional considerations. To develop a compelling argument about the causal influence of an intervention, the analysis must, first, provide a well-specified and credible rationale that links the causal mechanisms with outcomes; second, it must present evidence to substantiate the claim that the purported causal agent (the intervention) is itself a plausible explanation for the observed outcome; third, it must provide assessments of the diagnosticity and probative value of information about purported causal mechanisms and rival explanations. That is, we have to rule in or substantiate the basis for our conclusions through additional forms of evidence. The remainder of this chapter describes how the evidential base can be broadened and how diverse sources of evidence can be combined to strengthen causal inferences.

Broadening the Evidential Base

Initially, the experiment was an appealing way of testing the effects of interventions, in large part because of the conceptual simplicity of the process of developing and summarizing information. Evaluations following this perspective were approached as an input-output assessment. As such, developing an evaluation plan was relatively simple, entailing as it did the selection of suitable measures, the devising of an assignment plan, and vigorous management of the implementation of these key features. The synthesis of evidence on effectiveness was also straightforward. Inference about program effects was to flow from tests of statistical significance applied to data derived from randomized experiments. In essence, the development and synthesis of evidence about program effectiveness using the experimental paradigm implicitly mixes these two processes, thus removing any judgment on the part of the researcher.

Despite forceful warnings of inferential weaknesses (Campbell and Boruch, 1975; Cook and Campbell, 1979), quasi-experiments have been treated merely as impoverished versions of true experiments, the chief difference being the lack of random allocation to conditions. In contrast to the probing, searching, active testing of the plausible effects of rival explanations described by Campbell (Campbell, 1969, 1984; Campbell and Stanley, 1966; Cook and Campbell, 1979), the early studies seemed to be arrested at the point of trying to find approximate statistical models to control for influence of pretreatment differences. As Kenny (1975) pointed out, chance is only one rival explanation.

Two pitfalls are obvious. First, early quasi-experiments employed a very limited notion of what constitutes evidence about a program's effectiveness. That is, evidence of program effectiveness was limited largely to establishment of one fact: Did the treatment group outperform the control group? A test of statistical significance was usually put forth in support of a claim. However, several intermediate facts must be established before a causal claim can be justified. For example, Were the conditions necessary for change present? Was the appropriate clientele exposed to the intervention? Was the intervention properly implemented? Was the intervention implemented with sufficient intensity to trigger the necessary causal chain of events needed to induce a change in behavior? Each of these intermediate questions requires that we decompose the molar treatment package into its component parts. Judging form reviews of the literature (Lipsey and others, 1985), explorations inside the black box of program treatments are relatively rare.

Second, contemporary quasi-experimental analysis assumes a passive posture toward the development and synthesis of evidence about causal claims. This posture is manifest in three widespread beliefs: first, that nonequivalent group designs can and do control for threats to validity; second, that statistical procedures (for example, tests of significance, adjustments for nonequivalence) perform as intended; and third, that assumptions are robust enough to be safely ignored. In the main, this passivity leaves the impression that most quasi-experimental assessments are based on scientistic rather than on scientific principles. For example, the adequacy of the statistical design (for example, its statistical power, goodness of fit) is rarely considered, sensitivity analyses are rarely performed, and assumptions are often stated as caveats rather than being probed with additional design elements. These issues would have probably gone unnoticed had it not been for the work of secondary analysts (Bloom, 1984, Director, 1977; Murnane and others, 1985; Wortman and others, 1978).

Fortunately, the early narrowness exhibited in quasi-experimentation has begun to give way to increasingly comprehensive approaches that more closely resemble elements of the judgment process outlined in this chapter. This process has been operationalized in two ways: First, the evidential base for program assessment has been substantively broadened through the inclusion of mediational models and contextual factors. Second, program assessment has become more searching, probing, and critical through the use of multiple methodologies. These increasingly comprehensive approaches are particularly well represented in two types of quasi-experiments: structural models and what we will call "patched-up" designs. Each is sufficiently distinct to warrant separate consideration.

Structural Models. The classic input-output, black box orientation has been largely replaced by a structural modeling approach to assessment (Chen and Rossi, 1983; Judd and Kenny, 1981; Wang and Walberg, 1983). This approach represents a substantial augmentation of the basic two-group nonequivalent design. In part, it reflects a broadening of the types of "facts" that are needed if evaluations are to be useful (for example, needs assessment, program implementation, mediational links, client-by-treatment interactions).

Developing the Evidential Base. In one sense, prespecified causal models serve as a guide for the fact finder. To illustrate this point, contrast the old conception of quasi-experimentation depicted in the top portion of Figure 1 with the augmented model presented in the lower portion. Several features of the augmented version of quasi-experimentation characterize it as a system of inquiry that is very similar to the model described by Einhorn and Hogarth (1986) and as dissimilar to the input-output process of yesteryear. That is, in contrast to the impoverished model, the development of evidence within the augmented class of causal models entails modeling of the true pretreatment assignment processes; theory-based specification of outcomes in addition to policy-relevant ones; the modeling of exogeneous factors that influence outcomes beyond the intervention, thereby taking into account multiple causes and increasing the precision of the test of the intervention; modeling of factors that influence the receipt of treatment and mediational mechanisms within the treatment package; monitoring and measurment of treatment delivery systems (path c, integrity of program implementation); multiple measurement of all major latent factors; and ascertainment of the strength of the treatment as delivered (path $b \times c$) vis-à-vis theoretical prescriptions (path a).

What should be clear from Figure 1 is that these augmented models require the establishment of several interdependent facts. Further, these mediational models parallel the judgment models described by Einhorn and Hogarth (1986) and by Schum and Martin (1982). In program research terms, these models specify the need for developing and integrating evidence on the integrity of program implementation; its strengths; mediational mechanisms that link treatment receipt to program outcomes (contiguity and congruity); "true score" assessments of nonequivalence (that is, discounting); the credibility of causal interpretations; and the residual influence of exogenous predictors on the theory-based and policy-relevant outcomes (that is, covariation within the context of the causal field).

Synthesizing the Evidence. The structural modeling approach to quasi-experimentation depicted in Figure 1 provides a fairly straightforward means of synthesizing the multitude of information collected on each aspect of program inputs, process, and outcomes. The results of this analysis provide three types of evidence: primary evidence on the residual effects of the intervention on relevant outcomes (controlling for the effects of exogeneous factors), diagnostic evidence on the influence of critical structural parameters (for example, program implementation, receipt, and so on), and diagnostic evidence on the integrity of the methods and measures used to estimate each structural parameter.

For this approach, the synthesis process is largely a technical exercise. Further, simultaneous consideration of measurement and structural parameters overcomes some of the fundamental problems of more traditional, statistical techniques, such as analysis of covariance. With regard to model specification, the adequacy of the overall model can be diagnosed through several omnibus goodness-of-fit procedures (for example, chi square, goodness-of-fit index, and root mean square residual). Even if the initial model yields an inadequate fit to the data, Q-plots of normalized residuals and modification indices can help to localize the source(s) of the specification error. In this case, alternative hierachically related model specifications can be tested, and relative fit can be determined (Bentler, 1980).

The Role of Judgment. Although the array of equations, diagnostic tests, and procedures for guiding model respecification generated by this approach gives the impression of an objective basis for summarizing evidence on the input, process, and outcomes of interventions, obtaining a satisfactory fit of the data to the underlying model must be guided by theoretical or substantive considerations (Jöreskog and Sörbom, 1981). At the same time, handy diagnostic tests that pinpoint individual parameters that lead to poorness of fit can short-circuit the critical thought process associated with causal analysis (Cliff, 1983).

Limitations. A critical examination of the structural model reveals some strong similarities to its predecessor. Namely, the process of causal inquiry is rather mechanistic and inflexible. That is, the logic of testing rival explanations is buried within the statistical machinery. And, like its predecessor, it is

Figure 1. Two Views of Quasi-Experimentation: Then and Now

Part I: Outmoded characterization of Quasi-experimental analysis:

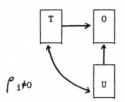

where: T is a dichotomous variable (received, did not receive)
        designating treatment status;

        O is the outcome;

        U is all other unmeasured causes of O and error, and

        $\rho_i \neq 0$ designates some degree of nonequivalence.

Part II: An augmented characterization of quasi-experimentation

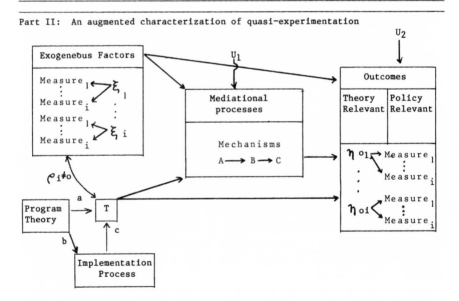

Source: Part II draws on Chen and Rossi (1983), Judd and Kenny (1981), and Wang and Walberg (1983).

not very adaptable to changes in the causal field (for example, changes in the program) or to unanticipated problems, and it does not illustrate the contingent nature of developing and synthesizing evidence that lies at the core of causal assessment via quasi-experimentation. This brings us to the second and perhaps more applicable type of multimethod quasi-experimental evaluation, which requires the piecing together of various forms of evidence to derive a causal conclusion. Here, the judgment process is highly applicable.

The "Patched-Up" Quasi-Experiment. Whereas the structural modeling approach may be able to overcome several key problems (for example, underadjustments due to fallible covariates), we should not lose sight of the fact that quasi-experimental analysis is essentially a practical approach to the acquisition of causal evidence. The analysis is meaningful and valid to the extent that a coherent set of facts has been examined and a pattern of evidence is plausible. As far as the actual conduct is concerned, the analyst is free to use whatever procedures are necessary or available to devise a reasonable test of the causal hypothesis. An examination of Cook and Campbell's (1979) recommendations for analyses that can be used in specific settings reveals numerous modifications and variations of familiar quasi-experimental designs, some of which represent simply the patching-up of designs previously considered to be uninterpretable. While the "patched-up" design is inelegant in appearance, it epitomizes the logic of causal assessment, and it is fairly consistent with the model described by Einhorn and Hogarth (1986). This connection has not been made explicitly in the literature on quasi-experimental analysis. When features of the judgment process have been exposed, the focus has been quite naturally on threats to validity.

An Illustration. Figure 2 provides a Campbell and Stanley–like description of the development of a patched-up quasi-experimental analysis. This design was originally conceptualized by Campbell and McCormack (1957) in an attempt to determine how military experience affected attitude change. As Figure 2 shows, the evaluation began with an inadequate research design—in this case a one shot case study. As time progressed and as new cohorts of trainees were tested and exposed to the military training, modifications in the design strategy were made. Thus, each element of the overall design served as a check on the validity of the other elements. Even though the individual elements of the design provided equivocal evidence, the effects of treatment were examined in several different ways, and therein lies the strength of the procedure. In this case, the validity of the analysis was contingent on the researcher's ability to demonstrate that the results were logically consistent across repeated cohorts of trainees.

Developing the Evidential Base. The Campbell and McCormack (1957) example highlights one key principle absent from the structural modeling approach that is compatible with Einhorn and Hogarth's (1986) notion of a complex scenario. Namely, testing the causal influence of a variable often

Figure 2. Schematic Representation of the Campbell and Stanley "Patched-Up" Analysis: The Institutional Cycle Design

Description of the Research Procedure	Schematic Representation of the Design Elements	History	Maturation	Testing	Instrument	Regression	Selection	Mortality	Selection X Maturation	Selection X
		Traditional Sources of Invalidity — Internal								
(1) One-Shot Case Study	Class A X O_1	−	−					−	−	
(2) Pre/Post, No Control Group	Class B_1 RO_2 X O_3	−	−	+	?	?	−	?		−
	Class B_2 R $\quad X$ O_4									
(3) Static Comparison	Class C $\quad O_5$ X									
(4) Appended Comparison (experienced)	O_6									
(5) Appended Comparison (no experience)	O_7									

Logic of the Assessment										
Comparisons: If $O_2 < O_1$ and $O_5 < O_4$ then		+	−	+	+	?	−	?		
Comparisons: If $\quad O_2 < O_3$ then		−	−	−	?	?	+	+		
Comparisons: If $\quad O_2 < O_4$ then		−	−	+	?	?	+	?		
Comparisons: If $O_6 = O_7$ and $O_{2y} = O_{2o}$ then		+								−

where X is the administration of the treatment;
        O_1 is the measurement of the outcomes of interest;
        R is the group assignment based on randomization;
        + indicates that the source of invalidity has been controlled;
        − indicates that this source of invalidity has not been controlled;
        ? indicates a potential source of concern;
        a blank space indicates that the source is not relevant.
        O_{2y} and O_{2o} represent a stratification of young (O_{2y}) and old (O_{2o}) recruits from Class B.

Source: Adapted from Campbell and Stanley (1966, p. 56).

requires the specification of conditional relationships. These conditional relationships appear as if-then conjectures about the nature of the program and the observable results: *If this set of processes occurs, we expect that outcome. If that result obtains, then either it was produced this way or that way.* This aspect of quasi-experimentation stresses the importance of establishing a line (or lines) of reasoning about program implications and the reasoning behind the methodological strategy. As Figure 2 shows, to rule out the explanation that "history" (that is, an external event unrelated to the intervention) was responsible for the outcomes, Campbell and McCormack (1957) relied on a conditional test. That is, if the treatment was responsible for the outcomes obtained, then the results obtained from O_1 (the posttest for experienced personnel) should be greater than O_2 (the pretest for new entrants), and O_4 (a posttest—only measure for the second cohort) should be greater than O_5 (the pretreatment measure for the third wave of entrants). Campbell and McCormack argued that this pattern of results would be more parsimoniously ascribed to the treatment (training) than to external events that would have had to appear consistently across replications and to influence all cohorts in the same way. Thus, the successful elimination of a source of invalidity requires specification of both the expected nature and the direction of its influence and generation of additional lines of evidence (in this case, assessment of multiple waves of trainees) that allow the analyst to assess the viability of the predicted relationship. Failure to disconfirm the notion that the treatment was responsible for the change via these "tests" results in additional confidence that the treatment is a plausible explanation for the observed outcomes, at least until such time as another alternative can be demonstrated to be more plausible.

Deriving tests of the implausibilty of rival explanations, as mentioned earlier, is only half of the argument. A comprehensive analysis must also rule in the plausibility of the putative cause. In the Campbell and McCormack (1957) example, this ruling in would involve several additional analyses to determine the strength of the treatment (that is, were conditions in the military environment really different from conditions in nonmilitary environments?), receipt of the treatment (for example, exposure, attendance), and comprehension. A good example of how evidence can be used to rule explanations in and out appears in Kutchinsky (1973). In a similar vein, Crano and Meese (1985) demonstrate how failure to consider whether individuals comprehend treatment instructions can influence estimates of effectiveness. In this case, efforts to understand the intermediate behavioral responses to an intervention uncovered a critical linkage between the treatment inputs and changes in energy conservation behaviors.

If we look at the literature on evaluation and applied social research carefully, we see several instances of research using this type of reasoning. In fact, some that have been given formal titles for example, the Solomon four-group design, stem directly from the application of the logic associated with patching up the inadequacies of other designs—in this case, the two-group randomized experiment was augmented with two posttest-only groups to assess the effects of pretreatment exposure to measurement. Other exemplars exist as well.

A classic use of if-then propositions served as the basis for the reanalyses conducted by Director (1978) and Wortman and others (1979). In both cases, the analysts supplemented the original two-group pre-post nonequivalent comparisons with an additional pretest. The logic here was simple but elegant. Given the uncertainty associated with the use of statistical procedures to adjust for nonequivalence, an additional pretest was used as a means of testing the adequacy of several different statistical adjustments. In essence, the argument was as follows: If nonequivalence between groups was properly accounted for by the statistical method under no-treatment conditions, then the resulting partial coefficients should be zero. A nonzero coefficient would be seen as evidence of biased statistical adjustment.

The Role of Judgment. The if-then inferences that appear within quasi-experimentation follow John Platt's (1964) strategy of strong inference, in which an attempt is made to explicate all reasonable explanations of the target situation (the causal field) and to extract the testable implications that discriminate among them. The resulting network of inferences guides methodological planning and generally requires methodological diversity beyond that necessitated by imperfect design components. These if-then inferences can be divided roughly into three types. Following Einhorn and Hogarth (1986), the first type concerns inferences and tests associated with program organization and activities (that is, the conventional process and implementation issues). The second set includes inferences and tests associated with the validity of the social theory embodied in the program concept. In both cases, these if-then statements are derived from the complex scenario that is composed of the treatment variable and other necessary conditions within a specified causal field. The third set of inferences and tests is associated with the methodology and circumstances of research (largely, rival hypotheses regarding causes of the outcome). Clearly, judgment plays a role, because it is involved in the articulation of expectations and in the interpretation of how well the observed pattern matches these expectations (Trochim, 1985). Note that the first two types of if-then propositions relate to the ruling in of the plausibility of treatment parameters as causal agents and that the third type is associated with conventional notions of the ruling out of rival explanations.

Multiple Methodologies. One aspect of quasi-experimental analysis that differs substantially from ordinary causal judgment lies in the fact that the analyst uses specifiable research procedures to gather evidence and sharpen the precision of the inference. Ordinary causal judgments are not necessarily based on a structured search for confirming and disconfirming information. However, the use of multiple cues and systematic rules of evidence is common to both types of assessment. For the scientist, there are numerous ways in which evidence can be gathered and used to derive causal inferences. In general, each way will be fallible in some respect, just as ordinary cues-to-causation are fallible. As such, it is generally recognized that the use of multiple cues combats the potential for erroneous inference.

Lipsey and others (1981) identified some generic techniques that could be used to diversify and bolster quasi-experimental evidence on treatment effects and grouped them into four categories: multiple measures, multiple research designs, multiple analyses, and supplemental data collection. Of course, each of these techniques entails several variations. For example, multiple measures can include measures that are intended to converge (that is, indicators that represent a latent variable) as well as measures that discriminate among constructs (that is, measures that are insensitive to the treatment but that can register changes induced by such artifacts as expectancy or demand characteristics). Further, not all measures are equally relevant, so a different a priori weight could be employed for each measure (for example, differentially relevant to the theory underlying the treatment plan). Note that in each case the analyst must make explicit judgments about the weights assigned to different measures. These weights should be grounded in program theory or prior evidence.

Multiple analyses of data also entail considerable judgments on the researcher's part. The potential diversity of practice here is quite substantial and controversial. In its simplest form, multiple analyses may involve post hoc disaggregation of evaluation data. For example, if process data indicate that the treatment was not properly implemented until a specified time, reanalyzing the data by disaggregating overall effects into early and late implementation phases is a sensible way of adjusting the causal field. To the extent that stratification is identified through other data, capitalizing on chance and regression artifacts are minimized. To the extent that post hoc stratifications are predicated on a defensible if-then statement, inference problems of the sort described by Leamer (1978) are lessened but not resolved.

Another generic method for broadening the evidential base entails supplemental data collection. This category of activities relies less than the others on human judgment in that it involves the conduct of new empirical analyses. These analyses can be directed at demonstrating the appropriateness of a specific statistical model (for example, by showing that change follows a fan-spread process in untreated groups of students), or they can be empirical tests of the sensitivity (or insensitivity) of specified measures.

Synthesis of Evidence. As elegant and tidy as the structural modeling perspective appears to be with regard to the synthesis of evidence, the patched-up analysis is inelegant and untidy. The tidiness of the structural modeling solution is principally due to the presence of a full matrix of data for all variables across all units of observation. For the patched-up analysis, this matrix is likely to be incomplete, and the result is that more judgment is required on the part of the analyst. While all the same rules of evidence apply, the process of synthesizing diverse forms of information is far more complicated, since it also requires the consideration of other potential problems (for example, data-instigated tests). As the multimethod portfolio becomes more diverse, the synthesis task becomes increasingly complex.

Einhorn and Hogarth (1986) specify a mixed model for deriving an overall judgment of the strength of a causal relation. Net strength is determined by discounting the weighted influence of rival factors. The validity of these judgments depends critically on the accuracy of the initial estimate of the strength of the X, Y relation and on the accuracy of the weights ascribed to plausible rival explanations. The same is true for quasi-experimental analysis. Each is subject to distortions, several of which are discussed in the next paragraphs.

Redundancy is one important potential source of distortion. A key feature of the multiple lines of evidence perspective on quasi-experimental analysis is the use of more than one way of examining program effects. Unless these methods are independent, the apparent convergence of the evidence can lead to overconfidence in the presence and magnitude of a causal relation. Some of the multimethod approaches that have been advocated are more susceptible to this problem than others. For example, mulitple analyses that rely on different assumptions cannot be considered independent because they rely on the same data. There is little additional probative value in such analyses if they converge. Further, contradictory results stemming from multiple analyses should not lower one's confidence unless there is reason to believe that none of the statistical models is appropriate to the data. Similarly, if multiple measures are not properly treated, they can yield unwarranted confidence due to redundancy. Failure to account for nonindependence among measures is quite common in meta-analysis. Strube (1985) shows that within-study redundancy among measures artificially deflates the size of the combined probability, and this inflates Type I errors substantially.

Differential sensitivity is another important source of distortion. Evidence is not always equal in its probative value. That is, some multiple design or measurement strategies will yield contradictory evidence because of technical inequalities. For example, the regression-discontinuity design is generally less powerful statistically than a randomized experiment of similar size. Different measures (for example, norm-referenced versus criterion-referenced) are differentially sensitive as indicators of change. This type of conflict is not easy to resolve. How to weight the evidence is a judgment call on the analyst's part.

The testing of null hypotheses is the last important source of distortion to be considered here. Often, testing the influence of competing explanations requires testing the null hypothesis. It is obvious that there are several ways in which the role of competing explanations can be underestimated. This in turn leads to overestimation of the net strength of the treatment hypothesis. As such, the probative value of the test of a rival explanation has to be established. This is a relatively uncharted territory, but several criteria come to mind. The threat needs to be plausible within the causal field established by the context. That is, demonstrating that a series of irrelevant rival explanations does not account for the observed outcomes cannot add credibility to the overall causal claim. The assessment must properly operationalize the theoretical concept embodied in the threat to validity. And, the analysis must be technically adequate. That is, it must be sensitive enough to have demonstrated the true influence of the rival explanation. Here, sensitivity entails sufficient statistical power as well as adequate measurement. Often, these criteria are not met. Space does not permit examination of other factors that may distort the synthesis of evidence. Given these simple examples, it seems reasonable to conclude that the literature on cognitive science and judgment could be illuminating.

Summary and Conclusions

The use of quasi-experimental analysis to assess causal relations has received mixed reviews. On the one hand, technical and conceptual solutions to knotty problems raise hopes that nonexperimental analysis will create a solid base from which causal inferences can be drawn. However, a look at the empirical literature suggests that it may be easier to specify the conceptual underpinnings of an adequate quasi-experiment than it is to carry one out. A recent review of the evaluation literature (Cordray and Lipsey, 1986) found no recent examples of the full structural modeling perspective depicted in Figure 1. Even simple patched-up designs are rarely employed (Lipsey and others, 1985).

The principle message of this chapter is that quasi-experimentation is a mixture of methodology and judgment. The literature seems to have ignored the role of judgment and to have superficially emphasized the objective features of the scientific process. Corrective solutions need to confront the fact that causal analysis within complex environments will require a more active assessment that entails reasoning and statistical modeling. Even in the best of cases, the veracity of the causal inference will be unknown. At the same time, professional decision makers, such as coroners and jurists, and the rest of us routinely make causal inferences about important aspects of our environments. Capitalizing on our strengths as information processors and understanding our limitations seem to offer a promising new direction for causal analysis in applied research.

References

Bentler, P. M. "Multivariate Analysis with Latent Variables: Causal Modeling." *Annual Review of Psychology*. Vol. 31. Palo Alto, Calif.: Annual Reviews, 1980.

Betsey, C. L., Hollister, R. G., Jr., and Papageorgiou, M. R. (eds.). *Youth Employment and Training Programs: The YEDPA Years*. Washington, D.C.: National Academy Press, 1985.

Bloom, H. S. "Estimating the Effect of Job-Training Programs Using Longitudinal Data: Ashenfelter's Findings Reconsidered." *Journal of Human Resources*, 1984, *19* (4), 544–556.

Boruch, R. F., and Cordray, D. S. (eds.). *An Appraisal of Educational Program Evaluations: Federal, State, and Local Agencies*. Washington, D.C.: U.S. Department of Education, 1980.

Campbell, D. T. "Prospective: Artifact and Control." In R. Rosenthal and R. L.

Rosnow (eds.), *Artifacts in Behavioral Research.* New York: Appleton-Century-Crofts, 1969.

Campbell, D. T. "Can We Be Scientific in Applied Social Science?" In R. F. Conner, D. G. Altman, and C. Jackson (eds.), *Evaluation Studies Review Annual.* Vol. 9. Beverly Hills, Calif.: Sage, 1984.

Campbell, D. T., and Boruch, R. F. "Making the Case for Randomized Assignment to Treatment by Considering the Alternatives: Six Ways in Which Quasi-Experimental Evaluations in Compensatory Education Tend to Underestimate Effects." In C. A. Bennett and A. A. Lumsdaine (eds.), *Evaluation and the Experiment: Some Critical Issues in Assessing Social Programs.* New York: Academic Press, 1975.

Campbell, D. T., and McCormack, T. H. "Military Experience and Attitudes Toward Authority." *American Journal of Sociology,* 1957, *62,* 482–490.

Campbell, D. T., and Stanley, J. C. *Experimental and Quasi-Experimental Designs for Research.* Chicago: Rand McNally, 1966.

Chalmers, T. C. "The Randomized Controlled Trial as a Basis for Therapeutic Decisions." In J. M. Lachin, N. Tystrup, and E. Juhl (eds.), *The Randomized Clinical Trial and Therapeutic Decisions.* New York: Marcel Dekker, 1982.

Chen, H. T., and Rossi, P. H. "Evaluating with Sense: The Theory-Driven Approach." *Evaluation Review,* 1983, *7,* 283–302.

Cliff, N. "Some Cautions Concerning the Application of Causal Modeling Methods." *Multivariate Behavioral Research,* 1983, *18,* 115–126.

Cook, T. D., and Campbell, D. T. *Quasi-Experimentation: Design and Analysis Issues for Field Settings.* Chicago: Rand McNally, 1979.

Cordray, D. S., and Lipsey, M. L. "Evaluation 1986: Program Evaluation and Program Research." In D. S. Cordray and M. W. Lipsey (eds.), *Evaluation Studies Review Annual.* Vol. 11. Beverly Hills, Calif.: Sage, 1986.

Crano, W. D., and Meese, L. A. "Assessing and Redressing Comprehension Artifacts in Social Intervention Research." *Evaluation Review,* 1985, *9* (2), 144–172.

Director, S. M. "Underadjustment Bias in Evaluation of Manpower Training." *Evaluation Quarterly,* 1977, *3,* 190–218.

Einhorn, H. J., and Hogarth, R. M. "Judging Probable Cause." *Psychological Bulletin,* 1986, *99* (1), 3–19.

Fennessey, J. "Social Policy Research and Bayesian Inference." In C. C. Abt (ed.), *The Evaluation of Social Programs.* Beverly Hills, Calif.: Sage, 1976.

Finney, D. J. "Problems, Data and Inference." *Journal of the Royal Statistical Society, Series A,* 1974, *137* (1), 1–23.

Gilbert, J. P., Light, R. J., and Mosteller, F. "Assessing Social Innovation: An Empirical Base for Policy." In C. A. Bennet and A. A. Lumsdaine (eds.), *Evaluation and the Experiment: Some Critical Issues in Assessing Social Programs.* New York: Academic Press, 1975.

Gilbert, J. P., Mosteller, F., and Tukey, J. W. "Steady Social Progress Requires Quantitative Evaluation to Be Searching." In C. C. Abt (ed.), *The Evaluation of Social Programs.* Beverly Hills, Calif.: Sage, 1976.

Jöreskog, K. G., and Sörbom, D. *Analysis of Linear Structural Relationships by Maximum Likelihood and Least Squares Methods.* Chicago: International Education Services, 1981.

Judd, C. M., and Kenny, D. A. "Process Analysis: Estimating Mediation in Treatment Evaluations." *Evaluation Review,* 1981, *5* (5), 602–619.

Kenny, D. A. "A Quasi-Experimental Approach to Assessing Treatment Effects in Nonequivalent Control Group Designs." *Psychological Bulletin,* 1975, *82,* 345–362.

Kutchinsky, B. "The Effects of Easy Availability of Pornography on the Incidence of Sex Crimes: The Danish Experience." *Journal of Social Issues,* 1973, *29,* 163–181.

Larson, R. C., and Kaplan, E. H. "Decision-Oriented Approaches to Program

Evaluation." In D. Baugher (ed.), *Measuring Effectiveness.* New Directions for Program Evaluation, no. 10. San Francisco: Jossey-Bass, 1981.

Leamer, E. E. *Specifications Searches: Ad Hoc Inference with Nonexperiental Data.* New York: Wiley, 1978.

Lipsey, M. L., Cordray, D. S., and Berger, D. E. "Evaluation of a Juvenile Diversion Program: Using Multiple Lines of Evidence." *Evaluation Review,* 1981, *5,* 283–306.

Lipsey, M. W., Crosse, S., Dunkle, J., Pollard, J., and Stobart, G. "Evaluation: The State of the Art and the Sorry State of the Science." In D. S. Cordray (ed.), *Utilizing Prior Research in Evaluation Planning.* New Directions for Program Evaluation, no. 27. San Francisco: Jossey-Bass, 1985.

Maltz, M. D., Gordon, A. C., McDowall, D., and McCleary, R. "An Artifact in Pre-Post Designs: How It Can Mistakenly Make Delinquency Programs Look Effective." *Evaluation Review,* 1980, *4,* 216–225.

Murnane, R. J., Newstead, S., and Olsen, R. J. "Comparing Public and Private Schools: The Puzzling Role of Selectivity Bias." *Journal of Business and Economic Statistics,* 1985, *3* (1), 23–35.

Platt, J. "Strong Inference." *Science,* 1964, *146,* 347–353.

Scheirer, M. A., and Rezmovic, E. L. "Measuring the Degree of Program Implementation: A Methodological Review." *Evaluation Review,* 1983, *8* (6), 747–776.

Schum, D. A., and Martin, A. W. "Formal and Empirical Research on Cascaded Inference in Jurisprudence." *Law and Society Review,* 1982, *17* (1), 105–151.

Shadish, W. R., Jr., and Reis, J. "A Review of Studies of the Effectiveness of Programs to Improve Pregnancy Outcomes." *Evaluation Review,* 1984, *8* (6), 747–776.

Strube, M. J. "Combining and Comparing Significance Levels from Nonindependent Hypothesis Tests." *Psychological Bulletin,* 1985, *97* (2), 334–341.

Trochim, W. M. K. "Pattern Matching, Construct Validity, and Conceptualization in Program Evaluation." *Evaluation Review,* 1985, *9* (5), 575–604.

U.S. General Accounting Office. *WIC Evaluations Provide Some Favorable but No Conclusive Evidence.* Washington, D.C.: U.S. General Accounting Office, 1984.

Wang, M. C., and Walberg, H. J. "Evaluating Educational Programs: An Integrative, Causal-Modeling Approach." *Educational Evaluation and Policy Analysis,* 1983, *5* (3), 347–366.

Wortman, P. M., Reichardt, C. S., and St. Pierre, R. G. "The First Year of the Educational Voucher Demonstration: A Secondary Analysis of the Student Achievement Test Scores." *Evaluation Quarterly,* 1978, *2,* 193–214.

Wright, W. E., and Dixon, M. C. "Community Prevention and Treatment of Juvenile Delinquency: A Review of Evaluation Studies." *Journal of Research in Crime and Delinquency,* 1977, *14,* 35–67.

David S. Cordray is group director for federal evaluation policy in the Program Evaluation and Methodology Division of the U.S. General Accounting Office, Washington, D.C. (The statements and opinions expressed in this chapter do not represent official U.S. General Accounting Office policy.)

Since it is usually the case that no defensible option for performing a task within quasi-experimentation is unbiased, it is desirable to select several options that reflect biases in different directions. This aim is to avoid constant biases and to overlook only those biases that can be considered least plausible.

Quasi-Experimentation in a Critical Multiplist Mode

William R. Shadish, Jr., Thomas D. Cook, Arthur C. Houts

The orientation to quasi-experimentation that we advocate in this chapter is a special case of a broad orientation to social science that we call *critical multiplism.* While our formulation of critical multiplism is recent, its logic is implicit not only in past work on quasi-experimentation (Cook and Campbell, 1979) but also in a great deal of related work (for example, Campbell and Fiske, 1959). Our first goal is to summarize critical multiplism. Detailed and self-critical discussions are available elsewhere (Cook, 1985; Houts and others, 1986; Shadish, 1986). Our second and major aim is to show how critical multiplism yields benefits when applied to some of the unique problems that quasi-experimentation faces. Thus, we shall not be concerned with tasks in quasi-experimentation that are common to all social science, for which critical multiplism also yields benefits—such as the program implementation and construct validity issues addressed by other contributors to this volume, such as Mark in Chapter Three.

Critical Multiplism

No single way of carrying out the subtasks in any scientific project is perfect, whether question formation, design, measurement, sampling, or the theoretical interpretation of results is at issue. Consequently, every effort

W. M. K. Trochim (ed.). *Advances in Quasi-Experimental Design and Analysis.*
New Directions for Program Evaluation, no. 31. San Francisco: Jossey-Bass, Fall 1986.

should be made to detect the full range of hidden assumptions and biases that are necessarily present in the particular options for conducting any intellectual task and to incorporate more than one option into the research design so as to vary the direction of presumed bias and thus avoid constant bias. When multiple options yield similar results, confidence in knowledge is increased. When different results occur, the analyst is left with an empirically based puzzle, but he or she is spared the premature conclusions that might have resulted if fewer options had been implemented in the research.

Campbell and Fiske's (1959) multiple operationalism is the most widely known and appreciated form of multiplism, and, since its justification is prototypical of all multiplism, it is instructive to review it briefly. Any single measure contains biases of different sorts. Investigators disagree about how a construct ought to be operationalized. Even when they agree, any single measure will contain some error variance and some systematic unique variance, and it will fail to include some components of the target construct. Multiple measures help investigators to note agreements and disagreements about how something ought to be measured, to discover empirical convergences, to note empirical discrepancies that can result from conceptual differences between measures, and to compensate for the error and variance unique to any particular operationalization.

These rationales need not be limited to the measurement domain; critical multiplism is in some ways simply a more global formulation of the kind of advice given by Campbell and Fiske (1959). Apropos to the present volume, quasi-experimental research requires that multiple tasks be performed, such as question formation, identification of threats to validity, construction of casual models, conduct of data analyses, and interpretation of results. Critical multiplism advises quasi-experimentalists to identify different options for each task, noting the strengths, biases, and assumptions associated with each option. When it is clear that no single option is perfect for a particular task and that several defensible options are possible, critical multiplism suggests selecting more than one option in ways that seek to prevent any constant direction of bias. The researcher then notes convergences and discrepancies between the results associated with different options, gaining confidence in casual inferences that remain dependable despite all the different biases believed to inhere across the analyses that are conducted.

Of course, it is not realistic to expect individual scientists to do all these things well. Scientists are limited in their knowledge of the tasks and options available and in their knowledge of the advantages and disadvantages associated with each. They have difficulty perceiving their own biases, and they are insulated from critical input by such irrelevancies as the academic disciplines in which they were trained (Faust, 1984; Mahoney, 1976). Critical multiplism acknowledges such limitations and advises researchers at all stages in their work aggressively to seek diverse sources of criticism of the choices that they are inclined to make, whether these sources be immediate colleagues, scholars with strong beliefs about the substantive topic at issue, results of past research, or competing theoretical analyses.

This call for multiplism necessarily implies that trade-offs and choices must be made. For example, to make *all* research tasks multiple would require resources that are rarely available. Fortunately, only those options need implementing that are likely to yield different results and that have been left homogeneous in past studies so that the danger of constant bias is real. Options also vary in cost. The less costly includes collecting multiple measures on the same subjects, having the same investigator use different models and assumptions to conduct multiple data analyses, submitting research proposals and reports to multiple critics, and studying the ways in which findings in other studies of the same topic that used different methodological options or theoretical perspectives have varied. It is usually more costly to sample multiple types of subjects, observers, and occasions, to hire multiple consultants for on-site visits, and to have different investigators conduct multiple analyses of the same data set. It is often prohibitively expensive to implement multiple independent studies of the same issue by different investigators at different sites. There can be little excuse for not implementing the options that are both presumptively important and less expensive and for not providing a public defense of decisions to implement particular research tasks in homogeneous fashion.

We have addressed these kinds of trade-offs and choices in the implementation of critical multiplism in somewhat more detail in past work (especially Houts and others, 1986; Shadish, 1986). However, thorough guidance is still needed for such tasks as selecting from among multiple options for a study, allocating between options within fixed budgets, and interpreting convergences and discrepancies that emerge in results from different options. Formulating this guidance is a major research agenda for those who find the critical multiplist perspective intriguing. In the present effort, we limit ourselves to illustrating such choices and trade-offs by example, since our purpose is to show concretely the practical benefits of applying critical multiplism to quasi-experimentation.

Quasi-Experimentation from a Critical Multiplist Perspective

Quasi-experimentation seeks to facilitate causal inferences about manipulanda, particularly in field research: it emphasizes use of control groups, use of multiple pretests and posttests, and knowledge of the treatment assignment process in order to rule out threats to the validity of causal inferences that follow from not assigning units to treatment conditions at random. Three prominent characteristics distinguish quasi-experimentation from other forms of social research. The emphasis on local molar causal validity (theory-centered conceptions of causation emphasize knowledge of generative or micromediating processes); the use of design features and statistical adjustments to compensate for the initial nonequivalence of treatment groups; and the relatively small number of units assigned to conditions in field research practice because of considerations of cost, availability, or logistics. A critical multiplist perspective implies that it is important to seek both to locate the sources and direction of constant bias that these features can engender and to identify ways of increasing the heterogeneity of quasi-experimental practice in order to reduce the likelihood of constant bias.

Three important points follow from a critical multiplist perspective on quasi-experimentation. First, a critical multiplist perspective implies that a one-sided commitment to the primacy of internal validity or local molar causal validity is not justified in quasi-experimentation, since noncausal issues are broached in such research, and other conceptions of causation can be probed in quasi-experimental work. In a critical multiplist mode, quasi-experimentation requires a thorough justification for the primacy of molar causation on a case-by-case basis.

Second, a critical multiplist perspective on the group nonequivalence problem implies that multiple design and measurement strategies can yield more accurate estimates of bias than can a single design or model. Quasi-experimentation requires multiple probes of a causal issue using diverse design features selected to result in heterogeneous substantive biases. The mere fact that a particular design was selected from a collection of possible quasi-experimental designs is no reason for assuming that valid causal inference is warranted. These designs are rarely unbiased, and in any case they do not cover all the research tasks involved in any piece of empirical work. Thus, there is no presumption that any particular quasi-experimental design succeeds in the crucial task of making heterogeneous the direction of all relevant bias. Similarly, since we rarely know the selection model that accounts for all the initial nonequivalence between quasi-experimental groups, no single statistical adjustment and no single model of the selection process can guarantee bias-free analysis. Quasi-experimentation in a critical multiplist mode requires multiple data analyses based on multiple causal models that make different substantive and statistical assumptions.

Third, a critical multiplist perspective on the units of analysis problem has similar implications. A single quasi-experiment is inevitably confounded with the special characteristics of the few local settings in which it is conducted. Quasi-experimentation in a critical multiplist mode would strive to integrate the results of individual quasi-experiments with the results of past research and with tests of any substantive theory relevant to the research issue, openly seeking for both convergences and divergences.

The three preceding paragraphs necessarily oversimplify complex matters, some of which we now elaborate in the three sections that follow.

The Causal Hypotheses

In Chapter Four of this volume, Campbell uses the term *local molar causal validity* to indicate an interest in the truth of statements about the existence of a causal relationship between manipulable treatments that can be brought under human control and effects that can be studied in naturalistic environments. To be interested in quasi-experimentation is to commit oneself, however tentatively, to this concept of cause. But, by considering some alternatives to each of the separate concepts subsumed in the global term *local molar causal validity,* one can see that other priorities about the guiding form of research question are possible.

First, quasi-experimentation prioritizes on validity, which is understood to be an imperfect approximation to truth about a real world that exists independently of human knowers. Some scholars would reject this prioritizing of validity, either because they deny that a real world exists or that it is worth studying (Lincoln and Guba, 1985), or because they contend that statements can be useful even if they fail to meet particular scientific standards (Wholey, 1983). Second, quasi-experimentation prioritizes on causality, but one can also prioritize on knowledge about the kinds of people reached by a treatment, on the quality with which the treatment is implemented, on the needs of clients, on the costs of services, or on the values implicated in program design (Lincoln and Guba, 1985; Rossi and Freeman, 1982). Third, quasi-experimentation prioritizes on molar causality, even though one can also be interested in more molecular causal statements that attempt to specify the components of a global treatment that are considered necessary or sufficient for a particular effect, the components of an effect that are most responsive to the causally efficacious components of a manipulandum, and the micromediating processes that intervene between the cause and effect covariation (Chen and Rossi, 1980; Cronbach, 1982). Finally, quasi-experimentation prioritizes on local causality even though evaluators can also be interested in the generalizability of the effects of the causal agents being studied.

These alternative emphases are often warranted, and they lead to case studies, sample surveys, implementation studies, structural modeling, and the construction of program models (Chen and Rossi, 1980). Indeed, most of the major debates in evaluation theory concern arguments for and against these different emphases (Cook and Shadish, 1986). Thus, quasi-experimentation and local molar causal validity are heavily emphasized by Campbell (1971) and Scriven (1980), who call for summative evaluations that describe the effects of social programs. However, other theorists defend other emphases. Some value molecular causal explanation over molar causal inference on grounds that the former fosters both generalizability (Cronbach and others, 1980) and the development of substantive theory (Chen and

Rossi, 1980; Weiss, 1978). Other theorists aim to produce whatever information they believe stakeholders want, irrespective of its links to causation (Stake, 1980; Wholey, 1983). They argue that routine emphasis on any particular type of question can so bias an evaluation that it fails to serve client interests. Since we do not know which of these emphases is right and since we have good reason to believe that each emphasis provides some unique and useful information about a social program, critical multiplism rejects a routine prioritization on local molar causal validity and quasi-experimentation in favor of a catholic approach under which local molar causal validity is only one question for evaluators, and its importance varies as a function of other factors (Cook and others, 1985; Shadish, in press).

Even when local molar causal inference is a priority, investigators can be interested in many variants of this theme. Researchers use verbal labels to represent the X's and Y's in the typical question, Does X cause Y? Usually, there is no single correct way of defining these components. For example, in his study of the causal relationship between equality of educational opportunity and student achievement, Coleman (1972) noted that he obtained different answers depending on the constructs that were studied and on the operations that were chosen—for example, when inequality was operationalized as the degree of racial segregation, or as race differences in school resource inputs, or as inequalities in intangibles like teacher morale, or as school inputs weighted by their presumed effectiveness in promoting achievement or when inequality of results was taken as prima facie evidence of inequality of opportunity. School quality can also be defined in many ways—as per-pupil expenditures, class size, teacher salaries, the age of building and equipment, or even the degree to which classrooms are quiet—and Coleman (1972) found that the impact of school quality varied with the definition that was chosen. This variation is especially problematic, since different stakeholders prefer different definitions of school quality and compete to have their own preferences used (Hanushek and Kain, 1972; Mosteller and Moynihan, 1972). Under such circumstances, multiplists advocate including all plausible operational versions of the research question that are likely to lead to different answers and to be of interest to some stakeholders.

Sometimes, practical constraints force individual research projects to run the risk of bias by conflating the causal question with the particular sample of constructs, methods, treatments, people, and sites that is feasible. In such situations, the investigator must make trade-offs between the causal question of interest and the practical constraints. For example, interrupted time series designs often require data from archives. Yet, in our experience variables are more likely to be archived if they tap distal, not proximal, outcomes, which means that investigators must limit their work either to suboptimal measures of a target construct or to an insufficiently comprehensive list of constructs. In this regard, Elinson (1974) has pointed out that information on infant mortality rates was most frequently available in the archived records of social programs designed to improve pregnancy outcome. But, rates are becoming increasingly insensitive as indicators of improvement, because they are now approaching their lower limits in the United States. Nevertheless, such rates continue to be widely used indicators, because they are available, even though floor effects may cause program effectiveness to be underestimated. In this case, the most feasible design does not closely correspond with the causal research question of greatest interest. When quasi-experimentation is conducted in a critical multiplist mode, it requires a guiding causal question to be asked in several ways, each of which taps a different bias. This requirement can easily lead to several substudies rather than to a single neat design—for example, to a time series study of a distal outcome concurrently with a nonequivalent control group design focused on proximal outcomes at a number of local sites.

It would be wrong to presume that a researcher interested in molar causation inevitably wants to construct the strongest causal inference possible. Some authors prefer as much reduction of uncertainty about causality as possible, arguing that it is critical to know how well an intervention works before suggesting long-term changes in support for it (Campbell, 1969, 1971). In this connection, Cook and Shadish (1982) argue that the absence of attention to strong causal inference in evaluations of the community mental health center program has left an unfortunate gap in our knowledge, since spontaneous remission could make the program appear more effective than it really is. Only an evaluation with stronger design features could probe this possibility and provide stronger causal inferences. However, one group of evaluation theorists suggests that strong causal inference is not always or even mostly appropriate. Wholey (1983) counsels evaluators to inform program managers both about the degree of confidence that they should place in a particular causal inference and about the additional studies that might be required in order to increase that confidence. It is then up to managers to decide whether they want to spend the sums required to increase confidence to a given level. As the long-term survival of Wholey's approach at the federal level suggests, his point may be valid. Managers do seem to want answers to a broad array of questions, and they sometimes make decisions with data that do not approach the reduction of uncertainty about causal inference to which social scientists typically aspire.

With so many possible types of questions and with so many variants of any one question, asking a single question of any kind can rarely be justified in evaluation. It is therefore crucial to seek criticism from friend and foe alike during the question formation stage so as to provide evaluators with at least some safeguards against systematic and perhaps inadvertent biases in the formation of the guiding evaluation questions.

The Group Nonequivalence Problem

A second distinguishing characteristic of quasi-experiments is their inability to equate treatment and comparison groups at the pretest. This would not be problematic if we could do two things: first, specify and measure the selection process through which different units were assigned to different treatments; second, specify and measure all the other theoretically irrelevant treatment-related forces that influenced outcome measures after a treatment had been implemented. Unfortunately, we can rarely if ever fully specify the true models either of the selection process or of the dependent variable. This makes the nonequivalence of treatment groups a perenially problematic issue for practitioners of quasi-experimentation.

In the absence of complete knowledge of the selection process, there is no single correct way of dealing with the problem of nonequivalence. To aid inference, statistical adjustments and improved quasi-experimental design features are often advocated. Statistical adjustments aim to provide more precise point estimates of the magnitude or probability of effects after adjusting for any measured biases confounded with treatment assignment. Design features add components to a study in the hope of better estimating no-cause baselines through the use of pretest waves or control groups, through systematic removals and reintroductions of the treatment, or through the addition of nonequivalent dependent variables (Cook and Campbell, 1979). But, while these features help to rule out such threats to local molar causal validity as regression to the mean, history, or selection, neither the statistical nor the design strategy completely solves the problem. Each has different strengths and weaknesses. Statistical adjustments require complete prior knowledge of the true selection process and valid measurement of all constructs entering into these models, while the emphasis on design features requires the valid estimation of counterfactual conditions that cannot be directly estimated because we cannot know what would have happened to units in a treatment group if they had not experienced their particular treatment.

For quasi-experimentation in a critical multiplist mode, the call is to search for any plausible constant biases that a single study or body of research may have left unexamined, given the substantive questions that were asked and the design features and statistical adjustments that were used. Note that a constant bias can result even if heterogeneous methods have been used, for it is the direction and not the source of bias that counts. Cook and Curtin (1984) give an example of this from research on the relationship between television violence and aggression in children. These authors claim that, despite a great deal of methodological heterogeneity, the predominant bias in all cases is toward exaggeration, not underestimation, of the effects of television violence. This conclusion was based on three presumptions: First, more powerful situational cues that elicit aggression were present in most past research than are present in the everyday life of children. Second, underadjustment may result from covariance analyses of survey data that attempt to take into account background differences between heavy and light television viewers. Third, television viewing measures are less reliable than aggression measures in panel studies analyzed using cross-lagged panel correlations.

Similarly, Shadish and Reis (1984) found apparently positive effects for social programs designed to provide food supplements or medical services aimed at improving pregnancy outcome and noted the heterogeneous collection of quasi-experimental designs that had been used. But, this heterogeneity masks the possibility of a constant overestimate of effects, because every study but one failed to determine whether patients in the program received care in other settings—a crucial omission, since there are now more than seventy federal programs that might improve pregnancy outcome in the United States. Since many of these programs are targeted at the same high-risk populations and since they are not coordinated with one another, it is plausible to think that each woman may be receiving additional services that can influence pregnancy outcomes. In the one study that did document the receipt of other interventions (Sharpe and Wetherbee, 1980), adding a food supplement to medical services yielded no benefits over and above those that could be attributed to the medical services alone. To resolve the doubt, it would not be sufficient to assess only the receipt of services directly intended to improve pregnancy outcome, since programs like food stamps and Medicaid may also have such an effect.

The search for substantive biases must go beyond mere methodism—that is, beyond the tendency to trust any single method to yield an invariably unbiased, or even least biased, answer. This caveat applies even to the randomized experiment itself. Cook and Campbell (1979) outlined some threats to validity to which random assignment is irrelevant, including resentful demoraliztion and compensatory rivalry. Although lists of such threats are useful in stimulating researchers to think of empirical substantive biases, they are dangerous if they encourage researchers to stop their search once the plausibility of the threats that have been listed has been discounted. Substantive biases are possible that have not yet been documented in texts on methodology. In this regard, consider a randomized experimental study of the effects of income subsidies to ex-felons (Berk and others, 1980). When the data were analyzed as coming from a randomized experiment, the subsidies did not affect major dependent variables, such as the number of subsequent arrests. Hence, structural modeling was used, and it suggested that the arrest rates may have varied as a function of the amount of money that ex-felons received—an aspect of treatment implementation that is imperfectly captured by the dichotomous group assignment variable of the randomized experiment. This difference helps to focus attention on a threat not yet fully discussed in treatises on validity—conceptualizing the treatment in a global, more molar fashion that attenuates estimates of what would result if the treatment were conceptualized in terms only of the causally efficacious components of that more molar treatment.

In many of the examples just cited, the use of multiple statistical adjustments and of quasi-experimental design features was haphazard rather than planned, resulting from investigators' interests, external criticism, and local conditions that favored the conduct of some kinds of studies over others. Critical multiplism aims to make multiplism a systematic part of research endeavors by encouraging investigators to consider ahead of time the options that they have available so they can incorporate the multiple measures required for any one statistical adjustment, make many adjustments, collect the data required for multiple designs, and identify fallback options that will later facilitate the interpretation of results if the planned methods prove infeasible.

The Units of Analysis Problem

In contrast to the characteristics of quasi-experimentation already discussed, the problem of the small number of units assigned to treatment is not an inevitable feature of quasi-experimental research. However, quasi-experimentalists are aggressive about conducting research in nonlaboratory settings, and it is often the case that few units are available in such settings for assignment to treatment and control conditions. The small number of units occurs most often when a treatment must be administered to a unit larger than the individual—for example, to the classroom rather than the student, to the entire community rather than to individual smokers, or to an entire state rather than to individual citizens (Campbell, 1969; Cook and Campbell, 1979). When there are few units, many biases can arise. First, subunits within the unit of assignment are not independent, and so they cannot be analyzed as if they were. Under most conditions, analyzing by subunits rather than by the original unit of assignment inflates the degrees of freedom, causes spuriously low estimates of standard errors, and thus produces too many statistically significant differences. But, analyzing by the original unit of assignment can dramatically reduce power when the sample size of aggregate units is low; thus decreasing the chances of detecting a statistically reliable effect. Second, rare or unique outside perturbations (local history) are more likely to influence a small number of units differentially than a large number is, and the interaction between treatment availability and treatment-correlated characteristics of environments is thus likely to have a disproportionate and theoretically irrelevant influence on results.

For example, in their three-community study, Farquhar and others

(1977) studied community education interventions for cardiovascular health. One community received a mass media intervention, another received the intervention plus face-to-face counseling for a random sample of high-risk patients, and a third community served as a control. This study is one of the milestones in this literature, and it has given the impetus to a distinguished ongoing tradition of community-based health promotion research. But, as a first study it suffered from difficulties that often accompany pioneering initiatives—and certainly the researchers' treatment of the unit of analysis is one such problem. Communities were the unit of assignment to treatment in this study, and so they should have been the units of analysis. But, since there were only three units, data analysis would suffer from the power problems just outlined. Thus, in many of their analyses, the authors treated individuals as the unit of analysis. Such treatment would be correct in analyzing some data from the total—for example, in subanalyses of the face-to-face counseling group in the second community or as part of a series of data analyses examining the stability of results under different sets of assumptions about the unit of analysis. But, to the extent that analyses with individual-level data form the sole or major basis for between-community contrasts, the analysis should be biased toward spuriously significant statistical conclusions about whether chance can explain the results.

Other issues resulting from the same problem are less easy to identify than the power issue, and it is difficult to know what direction of bias to expect from them. For example, in what ways did the communities differ from one another, especially as those differences might affect cardiovascular health? If, as Farquhar and others (1977) noted, the control community had a Spanish-speaking population (9 percent) that was only one half to one third the size of the Spanish population in the treatment communities (17 percent and 26 percent), we might want to ask whether Spanish and Anglo populations differ in ways that affect cardiovascular health and whether these differences could bias the control group to do better or worse than the treatment groups. In an effort to begin to answer these questions, the researcher in a critical multiplist mode would identify hypotheses about such matters as the major sociodemographic predictors of cardiovascular health and then search to see whether the communities differed on these predictors in a direction that would account for the study findings.

However, rather than relying on such post hoc criticism, critical multiplism is concerned with anticipating and minimizing the units of analysis problem in the early stages of a study. The list of design and measurement options that could be used for this purpose is longer than we can present here. Suffice it to say that design improvements and measurement strategies, when jointly applied, allow powerful causal inferences despite the small number of units entering into the analysis (Cook and Campbell, 1979). The design features include various nested and hierarchical options (Winer, 1971) that allow some assessment of the interaction between units and treatments; their feasibility depends on such matters as the number of units available and the extent to which communication about treatments or effects occurs between the units assigned to different treatments. Of great utility are crossover and ABAB designs, in which treatments are systematically applied to and removed from treatment or control conditions in order to probe whether an effect can be made to appear or disappear under the experimenter's control no matter which unit is treated or when the treatment is applied or removed. Also at issue are predictions about higher-order interactions and the addition of nonequivalent dependent variables that should be influenced by all known alternative interpretations other than the one under test. The point is that, if a complex a priori prediction fails to be disconfirmed, then few plausible alternative explanations are viable, no matter how many units are studied. Other helpful design features include adding more pre- and posttests both to assess existing trends and study the persistence of effects over time and to increase the number of degrees of freedom. The feasibility of each of these many options will vary from study to study, and in the examples that follow we illustrate some of the options available to quasi-experimentalists and some of the difficult trade-offs that must be considered when an option is used.

The ideal remedy is to increase the number of units by increasing the number of treatment and control sites. But, adding communities to a study like that conducted by Farquhar and others (1977) can be very expensive, and it may not be commensurate with such desiderata as isolating the cities from one another (Farquhar and others, 1984). However, it is sometimes possible to study random samples from within each unit and to use the resources saved by the sampling procedure to increase the overall number of units. This is often particularly feasible in educational research, where the number of classrooms can sometimes be increased by sampling some rather than all the students within each class. However, we doubt whether the three-communities study could have taken such an approach, for heavy financial costs were associated with establishing a stable treatment team in each community and with paying community media expenses. As a result, the cost savings for each individual dropped from the measurement plan at each site would be minimal when compared with the cost of adding a new site. Under such practical constraints, it is easier to add control communities, and in their subsequent five-city project Farquhar and colleagues (1984) increased the number of control communities from one to three.

If the number of units cannot be increased, sometimes crossover or ABAB designs can be used to introduce the treatment to the control condition at a later date or to withdraw and reintroduce the treatment to the original treatment groups themselves, thus replicating the study with the existing units. In this circumstance, a replicated pattern of results increases our confidence in the inference that a causal relationship exists. Applying this to the original three-community study suggests that Farquhar and others (1977) might have exposed their control community to the treatment at the end of the planned study period so as to see if it then caught up with the treatment communities. The crucial assumptions here are that the time needed for effects to occur is shorter than the period available for the study and that the costs of implementing a new treatment team can be borne. Alternatively, Farquhar and his team could have staggered the introduction of the media campaign in the second treatment community, for this would then have unconfounded the treatment and any general historical events that took place in the two communities.

These examples all involve the most expensive option of adding treatments or treatment sites. When problems of sample size loom large, it is usually less expensive to add measurements than it is to add sites or units. Farquhar and others (1977) did this in the original three-communities study with some salutary effects. Descriptive data suggest that the three communities were similar on such parameters as rural location, population size, and mean age. These data might also help those who want to begin assessing the potential generalizability of the study to, say, nonrural or predominantly black communities. (However, as previously mentioned, it would have been even more helpful for the authors to have assessed how these community characteristics were systematically related to cardiovascular health, for these are the relationships that might bias results.) The authors also added assessments of presumed causal mechanisms to aid in identifying and properly labeling those components of the treatment that were responsible for the effects claimed. These measures allowed them to discover that high-risk patients who received face-to-face counseling showed significantly increased knowledge of risk factors when compared with high-risk subjects in the same community who were exposed only to the media campaign. Given the close link between the content of the counseling and the new knowledge gained by high-risk individuals, the hypothesis that the treatment caused the knowledge changes becomes more plausible. Finally, the authors used measurement to show that the improvements in risk factors between the two treatment communities were virtually identical if one excluded the individuals counseled face-to-face—in effect replicating the treatment effect on a second unit.

Related measurement strategies include adding multiple pretest waves to assess existing trends in the communities prior to intervention. Even increasing the number of assessments on the same unit during the study improves the situation by increasing the degrees of freedom. So, Farquhar and others (1984) extended the five-communities study to nine years, with epidemiological assessments in each year in each community. They added four assessments of the same cohorts over time, allowing estimates of within-subjects variance that can be parceled out through analysis, thus improving the estimate of treatment variance. And, they also sampled four independent random samples over time, yielding an independent assessment of results. All this measurement helped inference, but it did not require increasing the major costs of the project by introducing new treatment sites.

Quasi-experimentation in a critical multiplist mode would try to use all these means of minimizing biases associated with the unit of analysis problem in order to show that those biases did not act in the same direction and that they were not unduly large. Nevertheless, no single study is likely to marshall the resources and skills needed to implement all these partial solutions. Therefore, an additional strategy is to rely on the accumulated results of multiple studies, each of which has different strengths and weaknesses, and to search for convergences and explain any divergences. For example, Farquhar and others (1984) suggest pooling the results of their studies with those from four similar programs of research around the country. While this suggestion is worth heeding, a critical multiplist perspective would leaven the suggestion with a caution against assuming that, because the studies in question were different in many respects, they have necessarily avoided bias that operates more in one direction than in another.

The growing interest in meta-analysis (Glass and others, 1981; Light and Pillemer, 1984), may implicitly reflect a recognition of the imperfections of single studies and the need for developing techniques that allow us to synthesize results across multiple studies. The benefits of this approach have been perhaps most prominent in the psychotherapy literature, where not only have multiple studies been meta-analyzed (Smith and others, 1980), but also multiple meta-analysts have studied the same literature from different perspectives and with different biases. This has produced some impressive examples of convergence on some conclusions, such as the now generally accepted conclusion that psychotherapy seems to work better than assignment to a no-treatment control condition (Smith and others, 1980) and the conclusion that paraprofessional therapists achieve outcomes comparable to those of professionally trained psychotherapists (Berman and Norton, 1985; Durlak, 1979; Hattie and others, 1984). The meta-analytic literature on psychotherapy outcomes also contains impressive examples of constant biases confounding interpretation that had not yet been detected. Thus, in the ongoing debate about whether cognitive therapy is superior to systematic densensitization (Shapiro and Shapiro, 1982; Smith and others, 1980), Berman and others (1985) showed that the apparent superiority of cognitive therapy in the Shapiro and Shapiro (1982) review may have occurred only because most of the studies that produced favorable results were conducted by investigators with an allegiance to cognitive therapy. Undoubtedly the final word has not been heard in many of these cases, but they offer clear examples of the potential benefits of a critical multiplist perspective.

Conclusion

From a critical multiplist perspective, quasi-experimentation resembles chess in several ways. Each chess piece has different strengths and weaknesses with respect to mobility and direction. Similarly, in quasi-experimentation no two kinds of design or analysis are the same; each is associated with a unique set of biases. In chess, no single piece is capable of winning the game by itself. Rather, the best chance of winning occurs when all the pieces work together, using the strengths of each to protect against the weaknesses of the others. Similarly, in quasi-experimentation no single approach will yield the "true" causal inference, but rather causal inference is converged on through the joint use of multiple approaches that select methods and analyses to complement each other and to compensate for the strengths and limitations of each. In chess, skilled players never apply the same game plan against all opponents. Rather, they tailor their game to the known tendencies of opponents to play certain kinds of offensive or defensive games, being prepared for unknown and surprising variations that might emerge during a particular match. Similarly, in quasi-experimentation skilled investigators never rely on the same analysis or design for all studies. Rather, they tailor the study to what is known about the kind of program being evaluated, to the idiosyncracies of the particular program being studied, and to the problems that emerge during the course of the study. Finally, judgments about who is an effective chess player are never based on just one game. Rather they are based on cumulative evidence obtained from different types of games waged with multiple opponents over multiple occasions. The situation is similar in quasi-experimentation: Judgments about local molar causal validity are never based on a single study. Rather, they are based on cumulative evidence obtained from multiple studies conducted in multiple locations by multiple investigators, each with different biases. Quasi-experimentation should be like chess: Both are games for thinking people, both require hard intellectual work, and both require long-term tenacity and commitment in order to succeed.

The quasi-experimenter is constantly engaged in a battle against the partial validity of the methods that are available. Hence, the investigator who puts his or her faith into the results of a single method or even a single study is doomed to a higher probability of error than the more patient and more patently fallible multiplist. In much quasi-experimental study in the social sciences, the best hope is to design single studies that implement tasks in multiple ways, to rely on heterogeneous programs of research rather than on single studies, to seek out colleagues and other scholars who want to criticize one's own studies, and to convince other investigators who might have different perspectives on the problem to conduct their own competing studies. Space constraints have prevented us from emphasizing the last two points, but details can be found in Cook (1985), Houts and others (1986), and Shadish (1986). Above all, quasi-experimenters need to be ever skeptical of the results claimed by their colleagues and to be tenacious in ferreting out constant biases that may have been left homogeneous in past research, however heterogeneous the designs seem to be at first glance. The task is awesome, and quasi-experimentalists need every tool at their disposal to diminish the uncertainty of claims about causal connections operating in the real world.

References

Berk, R. A., Lenihan, K. J., and Rossi, P. H. "Crime and Poverty: Some Experimental Evidence from Ex-Offenders." *American Sociological Review,* 1980, *45,* 766–786.

Berman, J. S., Miller, R. C., and Massman, P. J. "Cognitive Therapy Versus Systematic Densensitization: Is One Treatment Superior?" *Psychological Bulletin,* 1985, *97,* 451–461.

Berman, J. S., and Norton, N. C. "Does Professional Training Make a Therapist More Effective?" *Psychological Bulletin,* 1985, *98,* 401–407.

Campbell, D. T. "Reforms as Experiments." *American Psychologist,* 1969, *24,* 409–429.

Campbell, D. T. "Methods for the Experimenting Society." Paper presented to the Eastern Psychological Association, New York City, April 17, 1971, and to the American Psychological Association, Washington, D.C., Sept. 5, 1971.

Campbell, D. T., and Fiske, D. W. "Convergent and Discriminant Validity by the Multitrait-Multimethod Matrix." *Psychological Bulletin,* 1959, *56,* 81–105.

Chen, H., and Rossi, P. H. "The Multigoal, Theory-Driven Approach to Evaluation: A Model Linking Basic and Applied Social Science." *Social Forces,* 1980, *59,* 106–122.

Coleman, J. S. "The Evaluation of Equality of Educational Opportunity." In F. Mosteller and D. P. Moynihan (eds.), *On Equality of Educational Opportunity.* New York: Random House, 1972.

Cook, T. D. "Postpositivist Critical Multiplism." In L. Shotland and M. M. Mark (eds.), *Social Science and Social Policy.* Beverly Hills, Calif.: Sage, 1985.

Cook, T. D., and Campbell, D. T. *Quasi-Experimentation: Design and Analysis Issues for Field Settings.* Chicago: Rand McNally, 1979.

Cook, T. D., and Curtin, T. R. "An Evaluation of the Models Used to Evaluate Educational Television Series." In G. A. Comstock (ed.), *Public Communication and Behavior.* Vol. 1. New York: Academic Press, 1984.

Cook T. D., Leviton, L. C., and Shadish, W. R., "Program Evaluation." In G. Lindzey and E. Aronson (eds.), *Handbook of Social Psychology.* (3rd ed.) New York: Random House, 1985.

Cook, T. D., and Shadish, W. R., Jr. "Metaevaluation: An Evaluation of the Congressionally-Mandated Evaluation System for Community Mental Health Centers." In G. Stahler and W. R. Tash (eds.), *Innovative Approaches to Mental Health Evaluation.* New York: Academic Press, 1982.

Cook, T. D., and Shadish, W. R. "Program Evaluation: The Worldly Science." *Annual Review of Psychology,* 1986, *37,* 193–232.

Cronbach, L. J. *Designing Evaluations of Educational and Social Programs.* San Francisco: Jossey-Bass, 1982.

Cronbach, L. J., Ambron, S. R., Dornbush, S. M., Hess, R. D., Hornik, R. C., Phillips, D. C., Walker, D. F., and Weiner, S. S. *Toward Reform of Program Evaluation:* San Francisco: Jossey-Bass, 1980.

Durlak, J. A. "Comparative Effectiveness of Paraprofessional and Professional Helpers." *Psychological Bulletin,* 1979, *86,* 80–92.

Elinson, J. "Toward Sociomedical Health Indicators." *Social Indicators Research,* 1974, *1,* 59–71.

Farquhar, J. W., Fortmann, S. P., Maccoby, N., Wood P. D., Haskell, W. L., Taylor, C. B., Flora, J. A., Solomon, D. S., Rogers, T., Adler, E., Breitrose, P., and Weiner, L. "The Stanford Five-City Project: An Overview." In J. D. Matarazzo, J. A. Herd, N. E. Miller, and S. M. Weiss (eds.), *Behavioral Health: A Handbook of Health Enhancement and Disease Prevention.* New York: Wiley, 1984.

Farquhar, J. W., Maccoby, N., Wood, P. D., Alexander, J. K., Breitrose, H., Brown, B. W., Haskell, W. L., McAlister, A. L., Meyer, A. J., Nash, J. D., and Stern, M. P. "Community Education for Cardiovascular Health." *The Lancet,* June 1977, 1192–1195.

Faust, D. *The Limits of Scientific Reasoning.* Minneapolis: University of Minnesota Press, 1984.

Glass, G. V., McGaw, B., and Smith, M. L. *Meta-Analysis in Social Research.* Beverly Hills, Calif.: Sage, 1981.

Hanushek, E. A., and Kain, J. F. "On the Value of Equality of Educational Opportunity as a Guide to Public Policy." In F. Mosteller and D. P. Moynihan (eds.), *On Equality of Educational Opportunity.* New York: Random House, 1972.

Hattie, J. A., Sharpley, C. F., and Rogers, H. J. "Comparative Effectiveness of Professional and Paraprofessional Helpers." *Psychological Bulletin,* 1984, *95,* 534–541.

Houts, A. C., Cook, T. D., and Shadish, W. R. "The Person-Situation Debate: A Critical Multiplist Perspective." *Journal of Personality.* 1986, *54,* 101–154.

Light, R. J., and Pillemer, D. B. *Summing Up: The Science of Reviewing Research.* Cambridge, Mass.: Harvard University Press, 1984.

Lincoln, Y., and Guba, E. G. *Naturalistic Inquiry.* Beverly Hills, Calif.: Sage, 1985.

Mahoney, M. J. *Scientist as Subject: The Psychological Imperative.* Cambridge, Mass.: Ballinger, 1976.

Mosteller, F., and Moynihan, D. P. (eds.), *On Equality of Educational Opportunity.* New York: Random House, 1972.

Rossi, P. H., and Freeman, H. E. *Evaluation: A Systematic Approach.* (2nd ed.) Beverly Hills, Calif.: Sage, 1982.

Scriven, M. *The Logic of Evaluation.* Inverness, Calif.: Edgepress, 1980.

Shadish, W. R. "Planned Critical Multiplism: Some Elaborations." *Behavioral Assessment,* 1986, *8,* 75–103.

Shadish, W. R. "Sources of Evaluation Practice: Needs, Purposes, Questions, and Technology." In L. Bickman and D. L. Weatherford (eds.), *Evaluating Early Intervention Programs for Severly Handicapped Children and Their Families.* Austin, Texas: Pro-Ed, in press.

Shadish, W. R., and Reis, J. "A Review of Studies of the Effectiveness of Programs to Improve Pregnancy Outcome." *Evaluation Review,* 1984, *8,* 747–776.

Shapiro, D. A., and Shapiro, D. "Meta-Analysis of Comparative Therapy Outcome Studies: A Replication and Refinement." *Psychological Bulletin.* 1982, *92,* 581–604.

Sharpe, T. R., and Wetherbee, H. *Final Report: Evaluation of the Improved Pregnancy Outcome Program.* Tupelo: Three Rivers District Health Department, Mississippi State Board of Health, 1980.

Smith, M. L., Glass, G. V., and Miller, T. I. *The Benefits of Psychotherapy.* Baltimore, Md.: Johns Hopkins University Press, 1980.

Stake, R. E., "Program Evaluation, Particularly Responsive Evaluation." In W. B. Dockrell and D. Hamilton (eds.), *Rethinking Educational Research.* London: Hodder and Stoughton, 1980.

46

Weiss, C. H. "Improving the Linkage Between Social Research and Public Policy." In L. E. Lynn (ed.), *Knowledge and Policy: The Uncertain Connection.* Washington, D.C.: National Academy of Sciences, 1978.

Wholey, J. S. *Evaluation and Effective Public Management.* Boston: Little, Brown, 1983.

Winer, B. J. *Statistical Principles in Experimental Design.* (2nd ed.) New York: McGraw-Hill, 1971.

William R. Shadish, Jr., is associate professor in the Center for Applied Psychological Research in the Psychology Department at Memphis State University. He is interested in evaluation theory, metascience, and mental health policy.

Thomas D. Cook is professor of psychology at Northwestern University. He has written extensively about methodology and social program evaluation.

Arthur C. 'Houts is associate professor in the Center for Applied Psychological Research in the Psychology Department at Memphis State University. He is interested in the psychology of science.

Validity typologies can enhance our understanding of quasi-experiments, but they can also serve as blinders. We can go beyond the primary concerns of validity typologies by studying causal process and by being explicit about the reasoning that underlies our inferences.

Validity Typologies and the Logic and Practice of Quasi-Experimentation

Melvin M. Mark

Quasi-experiments and validity typologies are deeply intertwined historically. Campbell and Stanley's (1966) classic work popularized the concept of the quasi-experiment, the typology of internal and external validity, and the concept of validity threats. Indeed, learning the various quasi-experimental designs typically meant learning the validity threats that each ruled out; consider the first sentence of Campbell and Stanley (1966, p. 1): "In this chapter we shall examine the validity of sixteen experimental designs against twelve common threats to valid inference."

The connection between quasi-experiments and validity typologies did not end with Campbell and Stanley (1966). Cook and Campbell (1976) expanded both the validity typology and the discussion of quasi-experiments. Cronbach (1982; Cronbach and others, 1980) critiqued Cook and Campbell's preference for designs that emphasized internal validity and proposed an alternative validity framework.

In short, the history of quasi-experiments is intertwined with the

The author thanks Lee Cronbach, Chip Reichardt, Will Shadish, Bill Yeaton, and Bill Trochim for their helpful comments on an earlier draft of this chapter.

W. M. K. Trochim (ed.). *Advances in Quasi-Experimental Design and Analysis.*
New Directions for Program Evaluation, no. 31. San Francisco: Jossey-Bass, Fall 1986.

history of typologies of research design validity. The relationship is of far more than historical interest. Validity typologies help to determine the nature of research design in practice. For example, the emphasis on internal validity in Campbell and Stanley (1966) and later works contributed to the notion that randomized experiments were the ideal in program evaluation (Campbell, 1984; Cronbach, 1982). Moreover, a research design has often been judged unacceptable because the Campbell and Stanley (1966) typology indicated that it failed to control for some validity threat, even if the threat was not relevant to the case under study (Cronbach, 1982). Further, the validity typology provides the cognitive framework through which researchers understand the advantages and disadvantages of various quasi-experimental designs.

Thus, it seems appropriate to explore alternative typologies of the validity of research design as a lens through which to examine quasi-experimentation. The typologies of interest here are conceptual frameworks that organize the types of and threats to the validity of inferences drawn from the application of research designs. The present discussion thus can be differentiated from discussions of test validity. I focus largely on causal inferences, although one of the validity frameworks reviewed (Cronbach, 1982) does not.

This chapter begins with an overview of several validity typologies. The descriptions are necessarily incomplete, but they suffice for present purposes. Drawing on that overview, I present an integration of the validity typologies. In subsequent sections, I use the integrated framework to contrast the positions of Campbell and Cronbach. I then critique the current practice and logic of quasi-experimentation and suggest expansions beyond the primary focus of dominant validity typologies.

An Overview of Validity Typologies

Campbell and Stanley (1966) stands as the seminal work in the area of typologies of research design validity. It popularized the distinction between internal and external validity, which Campbell (1957) made earlier. Internal validity was defined as "the basic minimum without which any experiment is uninterpretable: Did in fact the experimental treatments make a difference in the specific experimental instance?" (Campbell and Stanley, 1966, p. 5). External validity, according to Campbell and Stanley (p. 5) "asks the question of *generalizability:* To what populations, settings, treatment variables, and measurement variables can this effect be generalized?" For each type of validity, Campbell and Stanley (p. 36) presented validity threats—*"plausible rival hypotheses* available to account for the data." Campbell and Stanley presented eight possible threats to internal validity (for example, history) and four threats to external validity (for example, interaction of selection and treatment).

Cook and Campbell (1976, 1979) subdivided internal and external validity; the result was a four-category typology and almost three times as many validity threats. According to Cook and Campbell (1979), one makes distinct judgments about whether two variables covary as operationalized (statistical conclusion validity), whether the covariation is causal (internal validity), how the operationalized treatment and outcome variables should be labeled (construct validity), and across what persons, settings, and times the relationship generalizes (external validity). Cook and Campbell (1979, p. 37) also provided a more explicit definition of validity than Campbell and Stanley: "We shall use the concepts *validity* and *invalidity* to refer to the best available approximation to the truth or falsity of propositions."

In work that takes a position similar to that of Kruglanski and Kroy (1976), Cronbach (1982) proposed an alternative validity framework that focuses on the elements of the inference that a researcher wishes to draw from research. Cronbach distinguishes four types of elements: units (for example, subjects), treatments, observing operations (for example, dependent measures), and setting (that is, the times and cultural conditions under which the study is conducted). Cronbach constructs acronyms with these four elements, and the use of upper and lower case in these acronyms is meaningful. Upper case UTOS refers to the particular domain of interest in the research, that is, to the researcher's definitions of T (treatment) and O (observing operations) and specification of the population of U (units, typically persons). Lower case utoS refers to the specific instances in a study, that is, to the concrete manipulation (t), measures (o), and subjects (u) examined. (Cronbach does not use S in the lower case, because S is "fixed" in the Fisherian sense and does not stand for a domain that the investigator attempts to represent.) Cronbach uses an asterisk to form *UTOS, to refer to a domain of application different from the domain that guided the research. In the case of *UTOS, the treatment, the units, the observing operations, the setting, or any combination of these can differ from the original UTOS that guided the research. Note that *UTOS can be narrower than UTOS, for example, when it concerns a subset of the population of original interest.

Cronbach concerns himself with two types of inferences. One, from utoS to UTOS (that is, from research operations to the domain that they were selected to represent), he calls an *internal inference*. The other, from utoS to *UTOS (that is, from research operations to another domain of interest), he calls an *external inference*. In Cronbach's (1982) usage, the terms *internal validity* and *external validity* refer to the trustworthiness of internal and external inferences, respectively. Cronbach's use of the term *internal validity* thus differs from that of Campbell and Stanley or Cook and Campbell, in that it involves generalizing from research operations (uto) to a conceptual domain (UTO). Cronbach's internal validity therefore involves Cook and Campbell's external (u to U) and construct (t to T and o to O) validity. Although Cronbach applies a traditional sampling model, he emphasizes credibility and persuasion in his description of validity: "Validity depends . . . on the way a conclusion is stated and communicated. Validity is subjective rather than objective: The plausibility of the conclusion is what counts" (Cronbach, 1982, p. 108)

Reichardt (1986) also proposes a validity typology based on the elements of an inference. Reichardt's formulation (p. 14) is that an "effect size ES is produced on dimension D for recipient R in setting S at time T by cause C." The effect size ES represents the size of the difference on dimension D between two states of nature (for example, one in which the cause of interest is present and one in which it is not). In Reichardt's formulation, this effect size is a function of five factors. Cause refers to the treatment or independent variable, dimension is the dependent variable, recipient refers to the unit(s) that receive the cause, setting refers to characteristics of the state of nature other than the recipient and the cause, and time refers to the time that intervenes between administration of the cause and measurement of the dimension. Reichardt's conception is that an effect size is a joint function of the cause and the other four factors (for example, if the recipient or setting is changed, the effect size may also change).

For Reichardt, validity depends on how accurately all the elements in his system are labeled. He shows how various threats to validity involve mislabeling of one or more elements, and he points out that in each case invalidity arises because, relative to the way in which the data were generated, the label is either too exclusive, too inclusive, or both. In addition, Reichardt explicates the mechanisms by which researchers can take threats into account.

An Integration of Validity Typologies

We can see the commonalities of validity typologies if we consider an abstract, generic statement of the contingent form likely to describe a causal relationship: *The treatment causes the effect for persons (or units)* X *in conditions* Y. (This generic causal statement could usefully be extended in two ways: It could include the time element, and it could be described more precisely in terms of effect size (Reichardt, 1986). These two improvements, which are discussed briefly later, are excluded here solely for the purposes of simplicity.) Figure 1 summarizes the correspondences between the elements of this generic causal statement and validity categories in the typologies just reviewed as well as those of Kruglanski and Kroy (1976) and Krathwohl (1985). (These correspondences are general in nature, and they may not well represent the subtleties of each validity system.)

The cases in which a typology combines two or more elements into a single validity category are illuminating, but limitations of space prohibit extended consideration. Suffice it to say that researchers should generally consider each of these elements. Indeed, the fact that each of the typologies refers in some explicit way to treatment, effect, persons X, and conditions Y

Figure 1. Elements of a Generic Causal Statement

Typology	The Treatment	Causes	The Effect	For Persons X	In Conditions Y
Campbell and Stanley	External validity	Internal validity[a]	External validity	External validity	External validity
Cook and Campbell	Construct validity of the cause	Internal validity[a]	Construct validity of the effect	External validity (persons)	External validity (settings and times)
Cronbach	U	U,T,O,S[b]	O	U	S[c],U
Reichardt	C	C[b]	D	R	S
Kruglanski and Kroy	G	if = then[d]	M	For any X	Subcategory of "for any X"
Krathwohl	Treatment	Basis of comparison, demonstrated relationship	Observations and measures	Subjects	Situations

[a]The concept of internal validity and its threats refers only to causal inferences when the other elements in the generic causal statement are at a low level of generalization. (See text for explanation.)

[b]This typology does not include a separate category for the causes element; rather, it incorporates cause as the accurate labeling of other element(s).

[c]Cronbach's S refers only to global, historical setting. Cronbach presumes that local setting is implied in selection of U.

[d]Kruglanski and Kroy define this element in terms of the causes element but describe it in terms of inferential statistics.

seems to suggest that these elements are critical components of inferences from research design.

In fact, it is probably more accurate to think of these elements as generally useful but arbitrary ways of thinking about causal relations. The most useful way of "slicing" the elements may vary across instances. For example, in some cases the selection of units (or persons) implies the selection of local setting (Cronbach, 1982), but treatments can often be delivered—with varying effects—in alternative settings (Reichardt, 1986). Further, sometimes it may be useful to differentiate setting further, for example, into the setting in which treatment is delivered, the local conditions of subjects' lives, and the global historical conditions.

Expanding the Causal Statement

The generic causal statement of Figure 1 does not itself adequately represent the nature of inferences drawn from research. It must be expanded to include two critical concepts: level of generalization and certainty in inferences. These concepts will help us to understand how the causes element is treated differently in the various typologies.

Level of Generalization. Level of generalization is incorporated in some form into each of the typologies reviewed here. For example, the concept underlies Cronbach's (1982) differentiation between utoS, UTOS, and *UTOS as well as Cook and Campbell's (1976) construct validity and external validity, which involve generalizing from the specific to the abstract.

The concept of level of generalization can readily be applied to the four elements other than causes in the generic causal inference of Figure 1. For each element, the lowest level of inference from research would involve exactly those instances observed in the research. For example, persons X would be the observed subjects. A continuum exists of higher levels of generalization, that is of populations or domains other than the operational one about which one wishes to draw inferences. It may often be useful simply to specify two other levels of generalization that corresponds to Cronbach's UTOS and *UTOS.

Certainty in Inferences. Figure 1 can also be expanded to include the degree of confidence or certainty that one has in a causal inference. For example, an inference that a program has some positive effect might be made with great confidence or with very little certainty.

The concept of certainty can itself be distinguished into two components: the range of effect size in an inferential statement and the subjective confidence that can be placed in the statement. For example, I might state that program A causes an increase of five to eight units on outcome O for persons X but have low subjective confidence that I am accurate. Alternatively, I might conclude that the effect size lies between −1,000 and +1,000 and have very nearly 100 percent subjective confidence, though the conclusion itself is trivial. I believe that there are several advantages to differentiating (un)certainty into these two components, as is done with confidence intervals, but for the sake of convenience I shall treat them here jointly.

The concept of certainty plays a role in most validity typologies. It seems to underlie Cook and Campbell's (1979, p. 37) definition of validity as "the best available approximation to the truth," and it is part of their statistical conclusion validity. Cronbach (1982) strongly emphasizes the role of uncertainty reduction in the selection and formulation of research questions. And, Reichardt (1986) explicates a logic by which researchers can attempt to reduce uncertainty. In their attention to certainty, these authors call into question the adequacy of our traditional method for estimating uncertainty, inferential statistics.

Inferential statistics are commonly used to estimate certainty about an inference (that is, confidence intervals are estimated). Although inferential statistics are based on a well-developed logic, their applicability to most inferences in evaluation is limited for three reasons. First, the underlying assumptions of inferential statistics—namely, those involving representative sampling—are rarely met. Certainly they are not met for the treatment element or the effect element, and when they are met for the person X and conditions Y elements, the desired higher-level generalization is likely to go beyond the population or domain sampled (Cronbach, 1982). Second, inferential statistics generally do not account for possible validity threats (other than random variation). For example, selection artifacts are a commonly plausible threat with bias of unknown size (Cronbach, 1982; Reichardt, 1979), and a traditional confidence interval does not incorporate such uncertainty. Third, particularly in quasi-experimentation, inferences may be derived from multiple sources, such as multiple analyses, comparisons made at multiple sites, or multiple lines of evidence (Cook, 1985; Lipsey and others, 1981; Mark and Shotland, in press). Traditional confidence intervals do not accommodate these multiple sources of evidence or our tentativeness about their relative importance. These factors lead to the recognition that, for the high-level generalizations generally of interest, some range other than a traditional confidence interval is necessary to specify certainty. Reichardt (1986; Reichardt and Gollob, in press) suggests that we need to develop "plausibility brackets" as such a generalization of traditional confidence intervals.

Cause and the Conflict over Validity Priorities

The validity typologies reviewed here disagree far more about the causes element than about any other element in our generic causal statement. As Figure 1 shows, the validity type that Campbell and Stanley (1966) and Cook and Campbell (1979) identify as the most important, internal validity, corresponds to this element. In contrast, the Reichardt (1986) and Cronbach (1982) typologies have no separate category corresponding directly to the causes element but rather incorporate it as the correct labeling of other elements. Focusing on this difference can help us to understand why Campbell and Cronbach seem to differ on the priority that should be assigned to internal validity.

The Causes Element. Campbell and Stanley's (1966) and Cook and Campbell's (1979) category of internal validity can be defined clearly with the present terminology: Internal validity concerns the accuracy of inferences about the causes element when all other elements are at the lowest level of generalization. Thus, internal validity concerns the making of accurate inferences about whether the treatment that was implemented caused the effect that was measured for the specific persons observed in the particular setting under study. For internal validity, the causes element should therefore be construed in the past tense, that is, as caused. In Chapter Four of this volume, Campbell clarifies this interpretation of internal validity as local and concerned with a particular place and time.

Cronbach (1982) has reached a similar interpretation. He notes (pp. 127–128) that Campbell and Stanley (1966) "define internal validity as pertinent only to an interpretation of a particular historical event. . . . Campbell apparently has always meant the term *internal validity* to refer to an inference devoid of generalization." Cronbach (1982) and Kruglanski and Kroy (1976) criticize this understanding of internal validity on the grounds that the concept of causality implies more than an inference devoid of generalization.

Campbell and Cronbach. The differences between Campbell and Cronbach's validity priorities seem to result largely from Campbell's emphasis on scientific inquiry) and Cronbach's on more immediate applied policy concerns. They also seem to make different assumptions about how to maximize certainty. In placing the priority on internal validity (Campbell and Stanley, 1966; Cook and Campbell, 1979), Campbell seems to assume that having confident inferences at a low level of generalization (internal validity) ultimately increases the confidence about higher-level inferences. This assumes "that the consequences of being wrong about causal connections are greater than the consequences of being wrong about other features of research design" (Cook and others, 1985, p. 761).

Cronbach (1982; Cronbach and others, 1980) questions this assumption. According to Cronbach, an emphasis on certainty about the low-level inference (internal validity) generally degrades the fit between the observed constructs and units (uto) and the constructs and units of interest in policy making (*UTO); this degraded fit in turn decreases confidence in the high-level inference that is germane to policy. Cronbach argues that evaluations should maximize not internal validity but relevance, that is, the ability to draw inferences about the˙*UTOS that is of interest in policy making. Cook and others (1985) discuss other differences between Cronbach and Campbell.

Unfortunately, it is impossible to resolve the conflict between Campbell and Cronbach without a well-developed technique for assigning certainty or plausibility brackets to inferences at a higher level of generalization. That is, we would have to be able to specify which of the following situations allows more certainty: the situation in which a causal inference is clearly warranted at a low level of generalization (strong internal validity), but one or more of the elements of treatment, effect, person X or setting Y is a poor representation of the higher-level elements of relevance to policy; or the situation in which all four elements are good representations of the higher levels of interest, but internal validity threats have not been ruled out, so the effects observed may be spurious.

One likely answer is that there is no simple answer. Campbell's approach seems preferable when a treatment effect is robust across variations in persons and settings, but causal inference is difficult because spurious relationships are likely. In contrast, Cronbach's approach seems preferable when spurious relationships are unlikely or can easily be ruled out, but a treatment effect is not robust. Unfortunately, the researcher is not likely to know in advance which conditions hold, at least without more substantive knowledge than we generally have. Thus, the dilemma remains.

Of course, when a causal inference about treatment effects is desired, it is preferable to avoid the horns of this dilemma by facilitating all forms of validity about research-based inferences, as both Cook and Campbell (1979) and Cronbach (1982) agree. Cronbach paraphrases Joe Garagiola's remark that in baseball good pitching always beats good hitting, and vice versa. In Cronbach's (1982, p. 331) view, "Comparability of groups adds more to validity than does representativeness, and vice versa."

Moving from Low- to High-Level Generalizations. To minimize the conflict just described, researchers must be aware of and use creatively not only the familiar techniques that strengthen internal validity (Campbell and Stanley, 1966; Cook and Campbell, 1979) but also procedures that enhance the validity with which high-level generalizations can be based on the low (that is, the operational) level. Both Cook and Campbell (1979) and Cronbach (1982) have offered suggestions aimed at strengthening the move from the lowest to a higher level of generalization. I believe that three principles or assumptions are implicit in these recommendations: a similarity principle, a robustness principle, and an explanation principle.

First, most of Cook and Campbell's (1979) and Cronbach's (1982) recommendations about sampling are based on a similarity principle, that is, on the assumption that one can predict from like instances. Campbell and Stanley (1966, p. 17) labeled this "the assumption of the 'stickiness' of nature." The similarity principle underlies both Cronbach's logic of representativeness and emphasis on those instances most like *UTOS and Cook and Campbell's (1979) random sampling and modal instance models for increasing external validity. (One observes a representative or modal sample at time X because one believes that doing so allows prediction to a similar population at time $X + 1$.) The similarity principle also underlies some recommendations about treatment and outcome constructs, such as Cook and Campbell's emphasis on careful fitting of research operations to the clearly explicated construct of interest.

Of course, the similarity principle is not foolproof. It assumes an ability to predict from instance to like instances. As Campbell argues in Chapter Four, similarity can be assessed on an infinite number of dimensions, and use of the similarity principle will lead to incorrect predictions if the analyst fails to note differences on a dimension that modifies the treatment effect.

Second, under the robustness principle, generalization is presumed to increase if an effect has occurred over diverse circumstances. (If the effect is not robust across heterogeneous circumstances, then one can fall back on the similarity principle and base predictions on the most comparable instances.) The robustness principle underlies Cook and Campbell's (1979) model of deliberate sampling for heterogeneity so as to increase external validity, as well as Cronbach's (1982) similar "extreme group design." The robustness principle also underlies calls by both Cook and Campbell (1979) and Cronbach (1982) for multiple analyses based on different assumptions, triangulation across multiple methods and multiple operationalization of constructs.

Use of the robustness principle does not guarantee accurate inference. The most serious problem is that one may wish or need to generalize to circumstances that differ in important—and perhaps unknown—ways from the diverse instances previously sampled.

Third, under the explanation principle, knowing why an effect does or does not occur allows prediction to future instances. The explanation principle is emphasized most by Cronbach (1982) who recommends observing and describing the linkages in program administration, treatment delivery, and client response as well as trying to discover the causes of the observed variability in effect size. Cronbach also supports attempts at explanation through the integration of findings with prior research and theory, a strategy emphasized by Krathwohl (1985). Cook and Campbell (1979) recognize the explanation principle but base few suggestions about research designs on it.

The explanation principle can, of course, fail to facilitate generalization if the explanation offered is inaccurate. But, how can we improve our explanation capacities? Perhaps the major way of facilitating explanation in evaluation is by studying causal process.

Studying Causal Process

By causal process I mean the mediational mechanism or causal sequence through which the treatment produces the effect. Knowledge of causal process implies substantial (and substantive) knowledge of the limits of generalizability (Cook and Campbell, 1979). That is, if we know the mediating linkages through which an effect operates, we also know many of the conditions required for the effect to occur. Thus, understanding process allows us to make increasingly confident high-level generalizations.

Each of the authors cited in Figure 1 discusses process to some extent, the most notable being Cronbach, who argues that process research can facilitate inferences about *UTOS. However, none of the typologies explicitly includes causal process, nor does any consider threats to the validity of an inference about process or methods for studying process in particular. Indeed, Cook and Campbell (1979) even seem to exclude causal process. However, both the validity typologies and the logic of causal inference (Reichardt, 1986) could be expanded to include research on process as a concatenation of causal questions. I will not focus on such an extension here: instead, I will review five alternative approaches that might be used to examine process.

The first, which is probably most familiar in evaluation, involves attempts to observe the process directly, as in Cronbach's (1982) advocacy of observing the linkages in program administration, treatment delivery, and client response. This model also underlies recent calls for implementation assessment and for looking inside the "black box" of the program. A variety of techniques have been suggested for observing the process, including causal modeling techniques (Judd and Kenney, 1981) and qualitative observation (Cook and Reichardt, 1979). While both qualitative and quantitative methods are likely to be useful in observing process, both approaches are essentially correlational, and the various threats to the drawing of causal inference from correlational data apply.

A second, more experimental approach to the study of process can be called the *blockage model*. This model is often used in biological research, particularly medical research. For example, if drug X is hypothesized to reduce depression by producing an opiate-like neural chemical, the researcher may inject half the subjects with a chemical known to inhibit opiate production and then give all subjects drug X. If drug X reduces depression in subjects who do not receive the opiate inhibitor, but it has no effect on subjects who receive the inhibitor, the hypothesized process model is supported. For a social science example of the blockage model, see Fazio and Cooper (1983).

The validity of inferences from the blockage model depends on the accuracy of the blocking agent. Obviously, if the blocking agent does not inhibit the mechanism that it is supposed to block or if the blocking agent has wider effects than anticipated, inaccurate inferences about process can occur.

The blockage model is often not applicable in evaluation research. Evaluators may lack either the necessary process hypothesis, an effective blocking agent, or both. Further, the blocking model is often unethical and uneconomical, for it requires providing the treatment while attempting to inhibit its effect. Nevertheless, researchers may wish to consider two possible forms of this model when a process hypothesis exists. First, laboratory analog studies might be conducted to obtain suggestive evidence of process. While analog studies have limited generalizability, they may enhance the total persuasive argument about the treatment and its effects (Cronbach, 1982). Alternatively, the researcher may search for naturally occurring blocking agents. Certain situational or respondent characteristics might function as blocks for a particular process.

An alternative to the blockage model is called the *enhancement model*. In the enhancement model, the researcher attempts to stimulate, rather than to inhibit, a hypothesized causal mechanism. For instance, in the case of drug X, the researcher would administer to some subjects a drug that facilitated the production of the natural opiate in order to see whether drug X reduced symptoms more in those subjects than in others who did not receive the opiate facilitator.

The enhancement model bears a clear relationship to the blockage model. In fact, the two could be combined, but they are not for pedagogical reasons. As one would expect given their similarity, the enhancement model shares most of the shortcomings of the blockage model, although it will usually be less ethically objectionable in program evaluation.

The *purification model* involves studying process by decomposing a treatment or outcome measure into its causally efficacious components. This approach, which is emphasized by Kruglanski and Kroy (1976), has been advocated for evaluation. However, it is perhaps best represented in the search for the "active ingredient" in medical treatments.

A fifth approach to studying process can be called the *pattern-matching model*. This model requires, first, that the researcher collect multiple observations; these will often be multiple dependent variables, but they could be data from various respondent subgroups, or settings, or times, or even treatment variations. Second, the process models under consideration must make different patterns of prediction (for example, process 1 predicts an increase for observations A, B, D, and E, while process 2 predicts an increase for A, B, and E with no change in C and D). Third, the researcher must compare the observed pattern with the hypothesized patterns. For an example, see the research of Cialdini and others (1978) on the process underlying "low-balling," a persuasion technique. See also Trochim's (1985) explication of several quasi-experimental designs in terms of pattern matching.

The logic of pattern matching can be expressed in general form. Indeed, it can be seen as underlying scientific inference in general (Campbell, 1966), including the other models described here for the study of process. However, there is pedagogical value in differentiating this from other models. It is worth noting that the pattern-matching model encompasses a familiar approach to the study of process, namely that of identifying the "active ingredient" in a treatment. Alternative ingredients constitute treatment variations, each with an implicit process theory.

The pattern-matching approach may often be useful in evaluation. However, it requires that specific and distinct patterns of predictions be derived from alternative process theories. Such specificity may sometimes exist (Trochim, 1985), but in many cases it may not.

This brief sketch has suggested five alternative ways of studying process. While these five ways share a common underlying logic (Campbell, 1966) and they can all be described in terms of the logic of causal inference (Reichardt, 1986), differentiating them may help to alert researchers to alternative strategies for the study of process.

It is important for researchers to recognize and pursue three general advantages of the study of process. First, construct validity, which is strengthened by process research, enhances internal validity, to use the language of Cook and Campbell (Trochim, 1985). That is, if evidence supports one causal process and rules out others, internal validity threats are rendered less plausible (Reichardt, 1986). This advantage is particularly important in quasi-experimentation, where internal validity threats may otherwise be plausible. Second, studies of process are an important technique for moving from low to high levels of generalization (that is, from internal to external and construct validity, in Cook and Campbell's terms, and from utoS to UTOS or *UTOS in Cronbach's terms). Third, understanding the causal process will in many cases facilitate the development of a more powerful or more efficient treatment (Cronbach, 1982). For these and other reasons, process studies are of major importance in evaluation. Such techniques as implementation assessment and pattern matching should thus be seen not as optional adjuncts to evaluation but as basic techniques fundamental to our attempts to derive the high-level generalizations that are typically of interest.

The Limits of Validity Typologies

As noted in the previous section, research on causal process has been underemphasized in most validity typologies. This section describes other shortcomings that may be basic to validity typologies.

Ignoring Validity Threats. Catalogues of validity types, lists of validity threats, and discussions of the threats ruled out by various designs serve as heuristics (Kahnemann and Tversky, 1973), that is, as cognitive shortcuts in judgments (Reichardt, 1985). They allow us to estimate the validity of inferences far more easily than we otherwise could. However, as with other heuristics they may sometimes lead us to incorrect judgments. That is, validity typologies, like other cognitive frameworks or theories, may act as blinders.

Reichardt (1985) describes an example in which a threat to valid inference was not recognized, probably because of the heuristic effects of previous validity typologies. Reichardt's example is an unusually creative study of teacher expectancy effects by Seaver (1973), which, as Reichardt astutely notes, plausibly suffers from a serious regression artifact unrecognized by the noted scholars who had reviewed the research favorably.

A similar alternative explanation can be applied to the cohort design with partitioning of the treatment. Cook and Campbell (1979) describe this design and illustrate it with a hypothetical evaluation of "Sesame Street." The study compared the kindergarten achievement test scores of siblings from two age groups: younger siblings who had seen "Sesame Street" before kindergarten and a cohort control group of their older siblings who were tested before "Sesame Street" was broadcast. The sibling pairs were stratified into two groups, depending on whether the younger sibling had been a heavy or a light viewer of "Sesame Street." A treatment effect would be evidenced as an interaction, with greater differences between the heavy and light viewers of "Sesame Street" than between the corresponding older sibling groups who had not seen "Sesame Street." According to Cook and Campbell (1979, p. 129), when this pattern of results occurs "it is difficult to come up with plausible alternative interpretations."

In fact, statistical regression can readily explain the hypothesized results. Younger siblings who self-select into heavy "Sesame Street" viewership are likely to be highly interested in learning, while those who self-select into light viewership are not. Given the less than perfect relationship between siblings' academic skills, we would expect that the older siblings would display less extreme behavior. The result of this regression effect would be a statistical interaction of the sort presented by Cook and Campbell (1979, p. 129) as an "interpretable outcome."

Why were the plausible alternative explanations overlooked in these two instances? Interaction findings, particularly of the crossover form found by Seaver (1973), are often difficult to explain, so researchers may be relatively cursory in their search for alternative explanations (Reichardt, 1985). Further, both Seaver's (1973) and the hypothetical "Sesame Street" studies differ in appearance from the research in which regression artifacts are typically discussed (Campbell and Stanley, 1966; Cook and Campbell, 1979). As a result, heuristic-based evaluation of validity might not lead to the consideration of regression artifacts.

Unnecessary Controls. The preceding examples illustrate that, through reliance on the heuristics of validity typologies, we may fail to recognize validity threats that exist. In addition, reliance on validity typologies can lead us to act upon the presumption of validity threats that do not in fact exist.

Cronbach (1982; Cronbach and others, 1980) argues that evaluators have often used unnecessary controls as a result of Campbell and Stanley's (1966) and Cook and Campbell's (1976) emphasis on internal validity. Part of Cronbach's argument is that experiments are sometimes implemented when causal inference is not of primary importance. But, Cronbach also argues that evaluators interested in program effects often employ control groups and other design features to rule out internal validity threats, even though the threats would not be credible in the absence of the controls.

Both Cook and Campbell (1979) and Cronbach (1982) agree that the plausibility of validity threats will vary across research areas and settings. Neither Cook and Campbell nor Cronbach would argue that chemists studying iron in isolated laboratories need a randomized control group to control for maturation. And, they would agree that there are some comparable circumstances in social research in which independent control groups are not required for causal inference. But, there seems to be disagreement about how frequent these circumstances are and about how researchers should in general proceed. Cook and Campbell (1979) seem to support the general use of design features that rule out validity threats, under the assumption that ruling out threats by design is preferable to ruling them out post hoc (but see Campbell, 1969). Cronbach seems to support a divergent position, namely that, given limited resources, design features should not be used to rule out a validity threat unless the threat is clearly credible in advance. For instance, Cronbach and others (1980, p. 290) state that, "when a study is being planned, whoever calls for a no-treatment control bears a burden of proof—the burden of making it plausible that practically significant change would occur in the absence of treatment."

This divergence of opinion, which in part harks back to the disagreement about validity and relevance, is difficult to resolve. However, it is important to note that the researcher's ability to foresee plausible alternatives may be limited. For example, not all history threats can be anticipated. Therefore, one might prefer to implement controls where possible in order to eliminate unanticipated validity threats. However, reasonable researchers will disagree about the value of doing this and the value of using resources in other ways.

The Ambiguity of Plausibility. The debate between Cook and Campbell (1979) and Cronbach (1982; Cronbach and others, 1980) about how to apply internal validity controls is even more difficult to resolve given the limits on plausibility as a criterion for assessing the applicability of validity threats. Cook (Cook and others, 1985) and Campbell (1969) certainly recognize that the plausibility of a given validity threat depends upon the research context and, further, like Cronbach they emphasize that the decision to invest in a particular control feature should be based on a thoughtful consideration of the trade-offs involved. Nevertheless, validity threats, which Campbell and Stanley (1966, p. 36) describe as "frequently plausible hypotheses," have largely been treated as generally likely counterexplanations. But, as Cook and Campbell (1979, p. 42) acknowledge, "in the last analysis, systematic research and carefully considered experience should influence the practicing scientist's concern about the likelihood of each of the threats we have identified and have provisionally labeled as plausible. . . . We anticipate that the threats . . . will be modified as experience accumulates."

The problem is that experience—particularly the systematic synthesis of research—has not yet accumulated to the point where we can confidently estimate the likelihood and magnitude of various validity threats. This problem is exacerbated in that validity threats are likely to operate in some contexts but not in others. For example, maturation may be plausible in compensatory education studies, but it is unlikely in research on computer skills programs in isolated Central American villages. While context dependency seems apparent in these examples, often it will not be, and more systematic evidence will be required to assess plausibility.

Indeed, it could be argued that one of the most useful developments for an applied social science would be the creation of a theory—or lacking that, an empirical estimation—of the plausibility of validity threats as a function of research question and context. An example of such needed research is Willson and Putnam's (1982) meta-analysis of pretest sensitization effects. Their review is useful because it estimates pretest sensitization for different types of research areas. While imperfect (it is limited to research areas where the necessary four-group design has been instituted), the resulting information is both more specific and more credible than a general intuitive notion of plausibility.

I should note that many validity threats cannot be assessed as directly as pretest sensitization (which can be estimated with a Solomon four-group design). Often reviews will have to focus on sets of threats, such as the internal validity threats that operate with the passage of time (for example, history, maturation). For an amalgam of threats, it would be possible to estimate the effect in one of two ways. First, one could compare effect size estimates for two research designs, one that was susceptible to the threats and one that was not (for example, a pretest-posttest one-group design versus a randomized experiment with pretest and posttest). Second, one could compare two effect size estimates derived from a set of studies having a single design with one estimate based on the full design and the other based on that part of the design which was susceptible to the threats (for example, one could estimate effect size as usual from a set of randomized experiments with pretest and posttest, and one could also estimate effect size omitting the control group— that is, acting as if one had only a pretest-posttest one-group design).

Such comparisons should be a standard part of research reviews, including meta-analyses. By seeing which specific threats or amalgams of threats seem to modify effect size estimates in which research areas, we may be able to reduce the ambiguity of plausibility.

The Arbitrariness of Validity Typologies. Kruglanski and Kroy (1976), criticizing Campbell and Stanley (1966) and Cook and Campbell (1979), point out that, while in the Campbellian framework treatment by subject population interactions are viewed as threats to external validity (that is, to the generalizability of the treatment effect across persons), such interactions could alternatively be viewed in terms of the construct validity of the cause or the effect. However, this criticism also applies to the other validity typologies, including that of Kruglanski and Kroy (1976).

This difficulty may arise simply because there is more than one valid way of stating a contingent relationship. Moreover, validity, in terms of truth value, may not be the criterion by which we can select between the two. Parsimoniousness, utility, theoretical relevance, or some other criterion may need to be the basis for choosing. The point is simple: A validity typology is not a foolproof, logically consistent, mutually exclusive set of categories. It is a device, an aid.

The Role of Validity Typologies. The authors of most validity typologies explicity acknowledge their limits. For example, Cronbach (1982, p. 77) notes that his validity "scheme [is] one of many possibilities . . . [A] writer emphasizing different points might introduce other elements." Cook and Campbell (1979, p. 39) "stress that [their] approach is entirely practical," based on the beliefs that researchers must address the questions corresponding to their four validity types and that "there are no totally compelling logical reasons for the distinctions."

As Campbell and Stanley (1966, p. 34) point out in their ground-breaking work, the purpose of a validity typology is to encourage readers to be more thoughtful in the design, analysis, and interpretation of research. And, as Campbell (1969, p. 355) has stated, scientific method is not "a dispensation from logic, prior to and external to science." A validity typology can greatly aid the evaluator who uses a quasi-experimental design, but it does not substitute for critical analysis of the particular case or for logic.

Other Recent Developments

Drawing inferences at the desired level of generalization, the importance of studying causal process, and the limitations of validity typologies can all be seen as recent themes in the literature on validity typologies. Other recent developments are examined in the paragraphs that follow.

Validity is not Relevance. To enhance validity does not guarantee that one's inference is of interest to the policy-setting community (Cronbach and others, 1980; Krathwohl, 1985). A researcher may attempt to maximize validity, but the results will be of little value if the research question lacks relevance (Reichardt, 1986). Thus, the issue of question formulation—an issue distinct from validity—is critical for evaluators (Cronbach, 1982; Krathwohl, 1985). Part of the recognition that relevance and validity are not isomorphic is the acknowledgement that the questions of primary interest in evaluation may not be causal questions, at least at many stages in a program of evaluation research (Cook and others, 1985).

Conceptualizations of Validity. Cook and Campbell (1979 p. 37) equate validity with an imperfect assessment of truth value: "We shall use the concepts validity and invalidity to refer to the best available approximation to the truth or falsity of propositions." In contrast, both Cronbach (1982) and Krathwohl (1985) equate validity with persuasion, credibility and consensus: "Validity is subjective rather than objective" (Cronbach, 1982, p. 108).

A related development is an increased awareness that validity is a characteristic of inferences, not of research designs or studies (Cronbach, 1982; Reichardt, 1986). Random assignment, representativeness, and so on are features by which we can often increase the validity of one of more elements of our inference and also increase certainty. Associated with this development is the recognition that "many strands of evidence and reasoning" (Cronbach, 1982, p. 170) may buttress an inference. (Also see Krathwohl, 1985.)

One can acknowledge that many strands of reasoning may buttress validity claims while retaining a truth value conceptualization of validity. Validity is, however, unknown (Campbell, 1974), while consensus is more tangible—but that does not require equating the two. However, some will argue that utility—that is, the ability to solve or at least to ameliorate problems—is a more important criterion than validity (Laudan, 1977).

Effect Size Versus Effect. Reichardt (1986) differs from the other authors of typologies reviewed here in that he formulates validity as a characteristic of inferences about effect size. Some other formulations at least appear to treat inferences from research as dichotomous yes-or-no decisions "about whether there is a causal reslationship" (Cook and Campbell, 1979, p. 38). But, treatments often have some effect, however minute it may be. Thus, it seems preferable to focus on effect size and on our ability to be certain that an effect size falls within some range of practical significance.

The Time Element. In his validity framework, Reichardt (1986) includes the time element, by which he means both the time when the treatment was implemented and the time when the effect was measured (and therefore the time elapsed between the two). Cronbach (1982) cites time as a feature implicit in his elements T and O. The importance of time should be obvious: A given treatment effect is not immutable; it is a function of time (among other elements).

Conclusions

The work of Campbell and Stanley (1966) and the others noted in Figure 1 has greatly enhanced our understanding of research. Validity typologies are valuable in helping us to understand quasi-experiments and in bringing potential validity threats to our attention. However, we can move beyond traditional validity typologies in several ways: by honestly acknowledging our certainty or uncertainty in an inference, by being explicit about the reasoning underlying our inference from a low to a high level of generalization, and by studying causal process. Moreover, we can be aware that the useful lessons of a validity typology do not substitute for critical logical analysis.

References

Campbell, D. T. "Factors Relevant to the Validity of Experiments in Social Settings." *Psychological Bulletin,* 1957, *54,* 297–312.

Campbell, D. T. "Pattern Matching as an Essential in Distal Knowing." In K. R. Hammond (ed.), *The Psychology of Egon Brunswik.* New York: Holt, Rinehart, 1966.

Campbell, D. T. "Reforms as Experiments." *American Psychologist,* 1969, *14,* 409–429.

Campbell, D. T. "Evolutionary Epistemology." In P. A. Schipp (ed.), *The Philosophy of Karl Popper.* LaSalle, Ill.: Open Court, 1974.

Campbell, D. T. "Can We Be Scientific in Applied Social Science?" In R. Conner and others (eds.), *Evaluation Studies Review Annual.* Vol. 9. Beverly Hills, Calif.: Sage, 1984.

Campbell, D. T., and Stanley, J. C. *Experimental and Quasi-Experimental Designs for Research.* Chicago: Rand McNally, 1966.

Cialdini, R. B., Cacioppo, J. T., Bassett, R., and Miller, J. A. "Low-ball Procedure for Producing Compliance: Commitment Then Cost." *Journal of Personality and Social Psychology,* 1978, *36,* 463–476.

Cook, T. D. "Postpositivist Critical Multiplism." In R. L. Shotland and M. M. Mark (eds.), *Social Science and Social Policy.* Beverly Hills, Calif.: Sage, 1985.

Cook, T. D., and Campbell, D. T. "The Design and Conduct of Quasi-Experiments and True Experiments in Field Settings." In M. D. Dunnette (ed.), *Handbook of Industrial and Organizational Psychology.* Chicago: Rand McNally, 1976.

Cook T. D., and Campbell, D. T. *Quasi-Experimentation: Design and Analysis Issues for Field Settings.* Chicago: Rand McNally, 1979.

Cook, T. D., Leviton, L. C., and Shadish, W. R., Jr. "Program Evaluation." In G. Lindzey and E. Aronson (eds.), *Handbook of Social Psychology.* (3rd ed.) New York: Random House, 1985.

Cook, T. D., and Reichardt, C. S. *Qualitative and Quantitative Methods in Evaluation Research.* Beverly Hills, Calif.: Sage, 1979.

Cronbach, L. J. *Designing Evaluations of Educational and Social Programs.* San Francisco: Jossey-Bass, 1982.

Cronbach, L. J., Ambron, S. R., Dornbush, S. M., Hess, R. D., Hornik, R. C., Phillips, D. C., Walker, D. F., and Weiner, S. S. *Toward Reform of Program Evaluation: Aims, Methods, and Institutional Arrangements.* San Francisco: Jossey-Bass, 1980.

Fazio, R. H., and Cooper, J. "Arousal in the Dissonance Process." In J. T. Cacioppo and R. E. Petty (eds.), *Social Psychophysiology.* New York: Guilford Press, 1983.

Judd, C. M., and Kenny, D. A. "Process Analysis: Estimating Mediation in Treatment Evaluation." *Evaluation Review*, 1981, *5*, 602–619.

Kahneman, D., and Tversky, A. "On the Psychology of Prediction." *Psychology Review*, 1973, *80*, 237–251.

Krathwohl, D. R. *Social and Behavioral Science Research: A New Framework for Conceptualizing, Implementing, and Evaluating Research Studies.* San Francisco: Jossey-Bass, 1985.

Kruglanski, A. W., and Kroy, M. "Outcome Validity in Experimental Research: A Reconceptualization." *Representative Research in Social Psychology, 1976, 7,* 166–178.

Laudan, L. *Progress and Its Problems: Towards a Theory of Scientific Growth.* Berkeley: University of California Press, 1977.

Lipsey, M. L., Cordray, D. S., and Berger, D. E. "Evaluation of a Juvenile Diversion Program: Using Multiple Lines of Evidence." *Evaluating Review*, 1981, *5*, 283–306.

Mark, M. M., and Shotland, R. L. *Multiple Methods for Program Evaluation Research.* New Directions for Program Evaluation, no. 34. San Francisco: Jossey-Bass, in press.

Reichardt, C. S. "The Statistical Analysis of Data from Nonequivalent Group Designs." In T. D. Cook and D. T. Campbell, *Quasi-Experimentation: Design and Analysis Issues for Field Settings.* Chicago: Rand McNalley, 1979.

Reichardt, C. S. "Reinterpreting Seaver's Study of Teacher Expectancies as a Regression Artifact." *Journal of Educational Psychology,* 1985, *77,* 231–236.

Reichardt, C. S. "Estimating Effects." Unpublished manuscript. Department of Psychology, University of Denver, 1986.

Reichardt, C. S., and Gollob, H. F. "Taking Account of Uncertainty in Estimating Effects." In M. M. Mark and R. L. Shotland (eds.), *Multiple Methods for Program Evaluation Research.* New Directions for Program Evaluation, no. 34. San Francisco: Jossey-Bass, in press.

Seaver, W. B. "Effects of Naturally Induced Teacher Expectancies." *Journal of Personality and Social Psychology,* 1973, *28,* 333–342.

Trochim, W. M. K. "Pattern Matching, Construct Validity, and Conceptualization in Program Evaluation." *Evaluation Review, 1985, 9,* (5), 575–604.

Willson, V. L., and Putnam, R. R. "A Meta-Analysis of Pretest Sensitization Effects in Experimental Design." *American Educational Research Journal, 1982, 19,* 249–258.

Melvin M. Mark is associate professor of psychology at The Pennsylvania State University. Coeditor of Social Science and Social Policy *and Volume 3 of the* Evaluation Studies Review Annual, *he is author of several chapters and articles on methodological issues in evaluation and applied social science.*

Confusion about the meaning of validity in quasi-experimental research can be addressed by carefully relabeling types of validity. Internal validity can more aptly be termed "local molar causal validity." More tentatively, the "principle of proximal similarity" can be substituted for the concept of external validity.

Relabeling Internal and External Validity for Applied Social Scientists

Donald T. Campbell

On the one hand, there have been widespread expressions of dissatisfaction with the distinction between internal validity and external validity and suggestions for its revision or elimination. In Cook and Campbell (1979), Tom Cook began a review of this literature, and he now has in preparation a much more systematic and extensive one (Cook, 1985; Cook and Campbell, in preparation). This chapter avoids that task.

On the other hand, both those who have enthusiastically adopted the distinction and those who oppose it, have most frequently redefined it to epitomize all the differences between pure laboratory experimentation and field tryouts of ameliorative programs. Are you, dear reader, perhaps one who has done so? Half of my own students fail to answer the following question correctly: When one adds a placebo control group in a pharmaceutical experiment, is this done to improve internal or external validity? As I read Campbell (1957) and Campbell and Stanley (1966), the correct answer is external validity.

This chapter is based in large part on the final report prepared under contract number SSN 552-12-4531 with the U.S. Department of Health and Human Services. The opinions expressed are those of the author and are not to be taken as government policy.

W. M. K. Trochim (ed.). *Advances in Quasi-Experimental Design and Analysis.*
New Directions for Program Evaluation, no. 31. San Francisco: Jossey-Bass, Fall 1986.

The meanings compiled in dictionaries are properly based upon usage, and the meanings ascribed to specialist terms are based upon usage in the relevant specialty. On these grounds, the term *internal validity* now means similarity to the pure treatment (rule-of-one-variable), fully controlled, laboratory experiment. Since that is not what we had in mind, we need to try again, with new terms.

It will help to remind ourselves of the dialectical motivation that lead to introduction of the distinction between internal and external validity. In the 1950s, the training in research methods that social psychologists received was dominated by Fisherian analysis of variance statistics, as though random assignment to treatment were the only methodological control that needed to be taught. (How the physiological psychologists kept alive an earlier model is a matter for another discussion.) In dialogue with this lopsided and complacent emphasis, we wished to point out that in out-of-doors social experimentation, there were a lot of threats to validity that randomization did not take care of and that the teaching of research design should be expanded to cover these other threats, which we classified as issues of external validity. It was against the overwhelming dominance of Fisher's randomized assignment models and an implicit, complacent assumption that meticulous care in this regard took care of all experimental validity problems that we were reacting. Thus, threats to external validity came to be defined as threats controlled for by random assignment to treatment. And, backhandedly, threats to internal validity were, initially and implicitly, those for which random assignment did control. This overlaps with the laboratory ideal, to be sure, but it excludes purity of the treatment variable. This was most nearly made clear by the inclusion of generalization to other treatments in external validity from the very beginning.

With my approval, Tom Cook has fuzzed up this simple distinction and added four threats to internal validity which randomization does not control (Cook and Campbell, 1979). It is symptomatic of problems with the concept that we now believe that at least one of these threats, resentful demoralization of respondents receiving less desirable treatments, if not all four, might well be grouped with construct validity of treatments. In the hypothetical case that Cook (Cook and Campbell, 1979) used to illustrate the threat, the posttest difference between experimental and control groups was a product of no change in the experimental group and entirely due to the resentful demoralization of the control group. In terms of the internal validity concept that I used in scoring the placebo-control-group item that I give to students, one could answer affirmatively the internal validity question, Did the experimental contrast as a total package in its specific setting cause a real difference? and relegate to construct validity (external validity in Campbell and Stanley, 1966) the question of how to interpret that validity noted difference.

In June 1984, Tom Cook and I spent three days planning a revision or new book. We tentatively agreed that *internal validity* needed relabeling. We went round and round on alternative labels. We are not satisfied with our present one, *local molar causal validity*, and it will probably not survive this chapter. The choice of terms is again due to the present stage of the dialogue. In continentalese, it has "historicist dialectical indexicality" (Campbell, 1982, p. 327). That is, the choice of terms is a product of the particular argument of this historical moment. *Molar* is used in specific reaction to the connotation of the theoretically "pure," "simple" experimental treatment. *Local* is used in reaction to a generalizability concept that may be a holdover from the logical positivist's so-called covering law model. Why the current rejection of positivism (in which, via Campbell and Fiske, 1959, I was a pioneer) should include covering laws I do not fully understand. Covering laws would seem like such nice things to have from any point of view on science. Perhaps it is that they implicitly require at the beginning of an inquiry knowledge that at best will only be available at completion (see also d'Andrade, 1986).

Local Molar (Pragmatic, Atheoretical) Causal Validity

For the applied scientist, local molar causal validity is a first crucial issue and the starting point for other validity questions. For example, did this complex treatment package make a real difference in this unique application at this particular place and time? By *molar* we connote recognition that the treatment is often a very complex hodgepodge (from the point of view of abstract analytic theoretical science), which has been put together by expert clinical judgment, not on the basis of the already proven efficacy of its theoretically pure components (main effects plus interactions). By *molar* we also connote an interest in evaluating this complex treatment as it stands, rather than first testing its hundred or so components one at a time, or in a hundred-variables-by-several-levels-each randomized ANOVA experiment. The molar approach assumes that clinical practice, participant observation, and epidemiological studies already have accumulated some wisdom, suggesting treatments that are worth further testing as molar packages. If these packages turn out to have striking molar efficacy, we will, of course, be interested in further studies, both clinically and theoretically guided, that will help us to determine which of several conjectured major components is most responsible for the effect. These later studies in turn will still be using complex packages, rather than testing theoretically pure variables in isolation or in experimentally controlled higher-order interaction. Pure-variable science can, of course, be a source of treatment packages (as in brain metabolite therapy for children diagnosed as potentially schizophrenic due to metabolite abnormality), but in preventive intervention these, too, will inevitably be a part of a complex social system of diagnosis and delivery. They will need to be tested as intervention packages under conditions of eventual application, or under facsimiles of such situations, that have been chosen both for clarity of scientific inference and for similarity to target conditions of application.

By *local* we indicate the strategy illustrated in pilot testing: Let's see if it really works in some one setting and time. If it does, later on we can explore the boundaries of its efficacy in other locales and with specialized populations. If it does not, we may be appropriately discouraged from further trials, even though it might conceivably work in some other setting.

While the molar local causal validity of the applied social scientist may be a far cry from the agenda of basic science, most of the problems of validity—and thus the methodology for the establishment of validity—are shared. Thus (if the applied research problem is not thereby abandoned), the two traditions of experimental control—experimental isolation and randomized assignment to treatments—are also ideal ways of establishing local molar causal validity. For applied ameliorative research under the field conditions of application, random assignment to treatments usually is the optimal approach to local molar causal validity, although not for external and construct validities.

Molar and *local* could both be taken as implying no generalization at all, conceptualizing a validly demonstrated cause-effect relationship that we do not as yet know how to generalize. The causal relationship would be known locally and molarly, but there would be no validated theory of it that would guide generalization to other interventions, measures, populations, settings, or times. This is, of course, an exaggeration. The theories and hunches used by those who put the therapeutic package together must, of course, be regarded as corroborated, however tentatively, if there is an effect of local, molar validity in the expected direction. Nonetheless, this exaggeration may serve to remind us that very frequently in physical science (and probably in social science as well) causal puzzles (that is, effects that are dependable but not understood) are the driving motor for new and productive theorizing. We must back up from the current overemphasis on theory first.

Basic scientists put a premium on clarity of causal inference and hence limit, trim, and change problems so that they can be solved with scientific precision given the current state of the art. Other causal hypotheses are postponed until the state of the art and theory development make them precisely testable. This strategy is not available to applied scientists. They should stay with the mandated problem, doing the best they can to achieve scientific validity but (in order to stay with the problem) often making use of methods providing less precision of causal inference where necessary. Thus, we applied social scientists need not only randomized experiments and strong quasi-experiments but also case studies, ethnography, participant observation, gossip collection from informants, hermeneutics, and so forth. Ideally, these materials will be used to provide the context necessary for valid estimation of the seriousness of the threats to validity and for valid interpretation of the results of formal experimentation, but if need be they may be used alone. We need these not because the social sciences seek a different kind of validity than other sciences do, but rather because to stay with our problems we must use techniques that, while improving the validity of our research, nonetheless provide less clarity of causal inference than would a retreat to narrowly specified variables under laboratory control. While using these techniques of the humanities, staying in real-world, nonlaboratory settings, the critical tools of threats to validity and plausible rival hypotheses are still central (Becker, 1979; Cook and Reichardt, 1979).

Relabeling External Validity

Even farther from stability or even transient consensus is a complementary reconceptualization of external validity. The following discussion, however dogmatic it may be, is a tentative and incomplete tryout of the principle of proximal similarity for that role. While that obviously will not quite do as a heading under which the present threats to construct validity and external validity fall logically, it may help to shake us free of past conceptualizations, as a way station en route to something more satisfactory. Here I move to this concept by stages.

Generalizing from the Local Without Representative Sampling. Akin to the relabeling of *internal validity* as *local molar causal validity* is a reformulation of the concept of external validity or generalizability set forth by Campbell and Stanley (1966). This has, of course, already been done by Cook (Cook and Campbell, 1979), who explicitly separated out and reconceptualized the issues of generalizing to other nonidentical treatments, now called *construct validity of causes,* and of generalizing from the outcome measures employed to other measures of effects, now called *construct validity of effects.* Remaining in the Cook and Campbell (1979) residual category of external validity is the validity with which one can generalize to other persons, settings, and times. Such generalizations should also be made on the basis of theory and thus they, too, should be reconceptualized as construct validities. That is, the validity of generalizations to other persons, settings, and future (or past) times would be a function of the validity of the theory involved, plus the accuracy of the theory-relevant knowledge of the persons, settings, and future periods to which one wanted to generalize (for example, to which one wanted to apply an intervention with demonstrated local molar causal validity).

This perspective has already moved us far from the widespread concept that one can solve generalizability problems by representative sampling from a universe specified in advance. Such an approach is obviously impossible for sampling from future occasions. However, the statistical technology and practical possibility is available for persons and for specified setting units, such as schools, schoolrooms, factories, hospitals, retail stores, cities, and counties. While national samples along these lines are often called for in evaluations mandated by Congress, it turns out that nearly all the high-quality scientific program studies (such as guaranteed annual income, housing allowances, school vouchers, coverage of psychotherapy by health insurance, and so forth) have chosen illustrative samples, exemplifying the target population in informal judgmental ways, employing samples of feasibility if not samples of convenience. For the New Jersey negative income tax experiment (Kershaw and Fair, 1976; Watts and Rees, 1977), the researchers gave the idea of a nationwide randomly selected sample of low-income households very careful consideration before deciding upon a few areas in New Jersey and a portion of Pennsylvania selected for both feasibility and theoretical reasons of an unquantified, general, and informal sort. I strongly endorse this approach. I believe it characterizes physical science as well as the most valid and useful of applied science.

This is, to be sure, an unpracticed ideal. But, it is so out of keeping with what we know of science that it should be removed even from our philosophy of science. A consideration of the time dimension will help to show that it is utterly unreasonable. In the physical sciences, the presumption that there are no interactions with time (except those of daily, lunar, seasonal, and other cycles) has proved to be a reasonable one. But, for the social sciences, a consideration of the characteristics of potentially relevant populations shows that changes over time (for example, a thirty-year comparison of college students) produce differences fully as large as synchronous social class and subcultural differences. To sample representatively from our intended universe of generalization would require representative sampling in time, an obvious impossibility.

More typical of science is the case of Nicholson and Carlisle. Taking in May 1800 a very parochial and idiochronic sample of Soho water, inserting into it a very biased sample of copper wire, into which flowed a very local electrical current, they obtained hydrogen at one electrode and oxygen at the other and uninhibitedly generalized to all the water in the world for all eternity. It was a hypothetical generalization, to be sure, rather than a proven fact. There have been by now many studies of the effect of impurities in the water upon hydrolysis, but these studies, too, have been based on very biased samples. The idea of a representative sampling of all the waters of the world, or even of all the waters of England, never occurred even as an idea. The very concept of impurities, of distinguishing the contents of water as "pure" stuff and alien materials, is one that would never have emerged had a representative sampling approach to water been employed. In the successful sciences, generalizations have never been inductive in the sense of summarizing what has been observed within the bounds of the generalization, but instead they have always been presumptive, albeit guided by prior laws. The limitations on generalization have emerged from efforts to check on an initial bold generalization in nonrepresentative ways. Scientists assumed that hydrolysis held true universally until it was shown otherwise.

In this light, had we achieved one, there would be no need to apologize for a successful psychology of college sophomores, or even of Northwestern University coeds, or of Wistar strain white rats. Exciting and powerful laws would then be presumed to hold for all humans or all vertebrates at all times until specific applications of that presumption proved wrong. We already are at this latter stage, but even here a representative sampling of species or school populations is not the answer. Theory-guided, dimensional explorations, as in comparing primates that vary widely in evolutionary development, are in the typical path of science (Campbell, 1969).

In program evaluation, I at least, recommend formal abandonment of the goal of nationally representative sample selection. Once there are interventions of such well-established effectiveness that the decision is made to adopt them nationally, sample census data on population distribution and sample censuses on schools, hospitals, or other distribution facilities to be employed and on labor and space costs can be employed for budgetary planning purposes. I do not anticipate that cross-validation of an intervention's effectiveness on a strictly representative national sample would ever be cost-beneficial or needed. If it were employed, it would be for administrative reasons, not for applied scientific validity.

The Principle of Proximal Similarity. The first presentation of external validity (Campbell, 1957) was entirely in terms of generalization to other treatments, measures, populations, settings, and times. As stated earlier, I feel we need something more appropriate than the generalization rhetoric and the solution of it by representative sampling from a universe designated in advance. This rhetoric is greatly reduced in Cook and Campbell (1979) through Tom Cook's notion of construct validity of causes and effects. In this shift, the validity of theoretical interpretation replaces atheoretical generalization to other treatments and measures. A shift has been made from a positivist phenomenalism to a fallibilist realism in which all treatments and measures are regarded as imperfect proxy variables for latent causes and effects.

But, even in this chapter, the rhetoric of "generalizing to" still persists, both in what has gone before and in what will follow. Somehow, I feel we need to preserve the valid aspects of our problem statement in a conceptual framework still more emancipated, still more characteristic of the coherence strategy of belief revision (Quine, 1951; Campbell, 1966, 1978), which we employ faute de mieux, even if we cling to a correspondence goal and meaning for the concept of truth. But, this chapter does not achieve that goal.

Under the principle of proximal similarity I would like to provide a metatheoretical basis for justifying a seemingly atheoretical rationale and approach to the generalization of findings. I do this ambivalently, because one of the attractive summaries of our new contrast is to regard local molar causal validity as atheoretical and construct or external validity as theoretical. Perhaps the principle of proximal similarity merely describes the route to theory-based generalization, given the multiattribute contexts with which we must begin and from which we can only be released by degrees of experimental isolation and control that are unaccessible in social settings.

While I believe that the principle of proximal similarity applies to pure science also, I want to make an argument for it specific to applied social science. In so doing I borrow from some earlier papers (Campbell, 1972; Campbell, 1973; Raser and others 1970). It was Harrod's (1956) effort to justify induction that moved me to this conceptualization. While I judge that he failed, as all such efforts must fail, his work introduces a profoundly different understanding of the presuppositions underlying scientists' efforts at inductive inference. For the earlier postulate that nature is orderly, Harrod substitutes the presupposition that nature is "sticky," "viscous," proximally autocorrelated in space, time, and probably n-dimensional attribute space, with adjacent points more similar (as a rule) than nonadjacent ones.

The most important practical justification of the principle (and of the need for confirming in practice the efficacy of social ameliorations) comes from the fact that our experience in generalizing social science findings shows that higher-order interactions abound, precluding unqualified generalization of our principles not only from laboratory to laboratory but especially from laboratory to field application.

It is most convenient to explain this in terms of the model of analysis of variance. Consider multiple dimensions of experimental variation A, B, C, D, and so forth, each of which occurs in several degrees of strength, with (in the simplest design) each combination of strengths being employed. (Thus, if there were four dimensions, A, B, C, and D, each of which had three strengths, there would be eighty-one different treatment packages. In addition to these treatment or independent variables, there is at least one dependent variable in terms of which the results of the treatments are measured. Let us call this X. For our present purposes, two major types of outcome need to be distinguished: main effects and interactions. If a main effect for A is found on X, then we have what could be called a ceteris paribus law: B, C, D being held constant at any level, the same rule relating A to X is found: For example, the more A, the more X. Where interactions are found, the relations are complexly contingent. For example, in an A–B interaction, there may be a separate rule relating A and X for each different level of B (for example, if B is high, the more A the more X, but if B is low, the more A the less X). Much more complex (higher-order) interactions can also occur, such as an A–B–C interaction in which the A-to-X rule is different for each combination of B and C.

Interactions, where they occur in the absence of main effects, represent highly limited and qualified generalizations. It is typical of the history of the physical sciences that many strong main effects have been found—generalizations conceivably true independent of time and place and the status of other variables. While eventually, in fine detail, the laws were found to be more complex, there was nonetheless a rich experience of discovering approximate laws of nature that could be stated without specifying the conditions on the infinitude of other potentially relevant variables.

There is no compelling evidence so far that the social sciences are similarly situated. If we take the one social science that uses the analysis of variance approach, experimental social psychology, the general finding is of abundant higher-order interactions and rare main effects. Even where we get main effects, it is certainly often due to the failure to include the additional dimensions (E, F, G, and so forth) that would have produced interactions. Frequently we are unable to replicate findings from one university laboratory to another, indicating an interaction with some unspecified difference in the laboratory settings or in the participants.

If such multiple factorial experiments can be regarded as experiments in generalization, they give us grounds for great caution, particularly when we generalize the expectation that, had we included dimensions E, F, G, and H or Y and Z in our experiment, the A–X relationship might well have shown interactions with some or all of them, too. The high rate of interactions on the variables that we have explored must make us expect something similar for the many variables that we have not explored.

Any given experiment can be regarded as holding constant at one particular level every one of the innumerable variables on which no experimental variation is introduced, each of which is like a single level of a potential experiment in which two or more levels of the same variable were systematically employed. We can guess with confidence that the farther apart the two values of B (or E or Z), the more likely it is that B will interact with the A–X relationship. (An empirical exploration of this might well be worth making. Data from complex experiments using three or more levels of a given treatment could be reanalyzed as two-level experiments, some as wide-range, using the two extreme levels and disregarding the intermediate, others as narrow-range, using adjacent levels from the original experiment.)

In anticipation of the outcome of such studies and in common with the intuition of most scientists, let us assume as a general rule that the larger the range of values on the background variable, the more likely these variables are to have strong interactions with the A–X relationship under study. Or, to put it more simply, as scientists we generalize with most confidence to applications most similar to the setting of the original research. When generalizing from our laboratory-based theory to a real-world social-ameliorative program, the values on all dimensions differ widely, and new interaction effects, as yet unexplored, become extremely likely.

Intuitively, we already use this principle of proximal similarity in many ways, and we can self-consciously use it in more. When it comes to disseminating a new ameliorative program of local molar causal validity, we will apply it with most confidence where treatment, setting, population, desired outcome, and year are closest in some overall way to the original program treatment. In contrast, for research on the limits of generalization, exploratory contrasts should be sought out for cross-validation that differ as much as possible from the first intervention in population, setting, and so forth while remaining within the legislatively targeted populations and problems. Purposive sampling for maximum exploration of generalizability on conceptualized dimensions will be substituted for a population-representative sampling.

In the new contrast, external and construct validities involve theory. Local molar causal validity does not. While this contrast is weakened in the principle of proximal similarity, I still want to retain it. The principle of proximal similarity is normally (and it should be) implemented on the basis of expert intuition. The use of the term *construct* in the expression *construct validity of causes and effects* (Cook and Campbell, 1979) may too strongly connote formal theory. Nevertheless, most philosophers or at least most logicians may well agree with Nelson Goodman (1972) that any concept of overall similarity is meaningless or incoherent, since there are potentially an infinite number of attribute dimensions on which such similarity could be computed. Our intuitive expectations about what dimensions are relevant are theory-like, even if they are not formally theoretical. Moreover, clinical experience, prior experimental results, and formal theory are very appropriate guides for efforts to make the exploration of the bounds of generalizability more systematic.

Nonconclusion

The material presented in this chapter is self-consciously inconclusive. It is a dialectical reaction, or overreaction. Let us hope that the overall iteration is headed for convergence.

References

Becker, H. S. "Do Photographers Tell the Truth?" In T. D. Cook and C. S. Reichardt (eds.), *Qualitative and Quantitative Methods in Evaluation Research.* Vol. 1. Beverly Hills, Calif.: Sage, 1979.

Campbell, D. T. "Factors Relevant to the Validity of Experiments in Social Settings." *Psychological Bulletin,* 1957, *54,* 297–312.

Campbell, D. T. "Pattern Matching as an Essential in Distal Knowing." In K. R. Hammond (ed.), *The Psychology of Egon Brunswik.* New York: Holt, Rinehart and Winston, 1966.

Campbell, D. T. "Prospective: Artifact and Control." In R. Rosenthal and R. Rosnow (eds.), *Artifact in Behavior Research.* New York: Academic Press, 1969.

Campbell, D. T. "Herskovits, Cultural Relativism, and Metascience." In M. J. Herskovits, *Cultural Relativism.* New York: Random House, 1972.

Campbell, D. T. "The Social Scientist as Methodological Servant of the Experimenting Society." *Policy Studies Journal,* 1973, *2,* 72–75.

Campbell, D. T. "Qualitative Knowing in Action Research." In M. Brenner, P. Marsh, and M. Brenner (eds.), *The Social Contexts of Method.* London: Croon Helm, 1978.

Campbell D. T. "Experiments as Arguments." *Knowlege: Creation, Diffusion, Utilization,* 1982, *3,* 327–337.

Campbell, D. T. and Fiske, D. W. "Convergent and Discriminant Validation by the Multitrait-Multimethod Matrix." *Psychological Bulletin,* 1959, *56,* 81–105.

Campbell, D. T., and Stanley, J. C. *Experimental and Quasi-Experimental Designs for Research.* Chicago: Rand McNally, 1966.

Cook, T. D. "Recent Attacks on Well-Known Validity Distinctions: An Appreciative Rejoinder." Paper presented at the annual convention of the Midwestern Psychological Association, Chicago, May 3, 1985.

Cook, T. D., and Campbell, D. T. *Quasi-Experimentation: Design and Analysis for Field Settings.* Boston: Houghton Mifflin, 1979.

Cook, T. D., and Campbell, D. T. "Quasi-Experimental Research: Conceptual and Design Issues After a Quarter Century of Practice and Criticism," forthcoming.

Cook T. D., and Reichardt, C. S. *Qualitative and Quantitative Methods in Evaluation Research.* Beverly Hills, Calif.: Sage, 1979.

D'Andrade, R. "Three Scientific World Views and the Covering Law Model." In D. W. Fiske and R. A. Shweder (eds.), *Metatheory in Social Science.* Chicago: University of Chicago Press, 1986.

Goodman, N. "Likeness." In N. Goodman (ed.), *Problems and Projects.* Indianapolis, Ind: Bobbs-Merrill, 1972.

Harrod, R. F. *Foundations of Inductive Logic.* London: Macmillan, 1956.

Kershaw, D., and Fair, J. *The New Jersey Income Maintenance Experiment,* Vol. 1: *Operations, Surveys, and Administration,* New York: Academic Press, 1976.

Quine, W. V. "Two Dogmas of Empiricism." *Philosophical Review,* 1951, *60,* 20–43.

Raser, J. R., Campbell, D. T., and Chadwick, R. W. "Gaming and Simulation for Developing Theory Relevant to International Relations." *General Systems Research.* Vol. 15. Ann Arbor, Mich.: Society for General Systems Research, 1970.

Watts, H. W., and Rees, A. (eds.). *The New Jersey Income Maintenance Experiment.* Vol. 2: *Labor-Supply Responses.* Vol. 3: *Expenditures, Health, and Social Behavior and the Quality of the Evidence.* New York: Academic Press, 1977.

Donald T. Campbell is past president of the American Psychological Association; member of the National Academy of Sciences; professor of social relations, psychology, and education at Lehigh University; and recipient in 1977 of the Myrdal Prize in Science of the Evaluation Research Society.

Modeling the process by which participants are selected into groups, rather than adjusting for preexisting group differences, provides the basis for several new approaches to the analysis of data from nonrandomized studies.

New Developments in Selection Modeling for Quasi-Experimentation

David Rindskopf

Until recently, most research on the analysis of data from studies with nonequivalent groups concentrated on adjusting the outcome for initial differences between or among the groups. Advances in these methods came primarily in the development of latent variable models so that adjustments could be made for initial differences in underlying (as opposed to observed) characteristics. Now, however, a new set of techniques has been developed that approach the problem differently. These techniques attempt to remove bias in the estimation of treatment effects by modeling the process by which participants in a study are selected into groups. This chapter describes these new methods, discusses the assumptions that must be met in order for them to remove bias, and describes how to find out more about them and the computer programs necessary to use them.

The example of selection modeling with which most evaluation researchers will be familiar is the regression-discontinuity design (see Trochim, 1984). In this design, participants are ranked on a quantitative variable, X. All those who score on one side of a chosen cutpoint on X are placed in the experimental group, and the rest are placed in the control group. Multiple regression can be used to analyze data from this design. If

W. M. K. Trochim (ed.). *Advances in Quasi-Experimental Design and Analysis.*
New Directions for Program Evaluation, no. 31. San Francisco: Jossey-Bass, Fall 1986.

the linear regression model is correct, there is no bias in the estimate of treatment effect, even though the groups are as unequal as possible at the start of the study, and there is no control for unreliability in X. Because X is the only basis for selection into groups and because X is used as a covariate in the analysis, there is no bias in the estimate of treatment effects.

What the analyst must worry about (and it is not a small thing) is whether the regression model that relates the outcome to X and treatment is correctly specified. If there is a polynomial relation between outcome and X, or some other nonlinear relationship, or if there are interactions that are not included, then bias can result. The assumptions of this model are much easier to examine than the assumptions of the models that will be presented later, because in this case we know exactly how people were assigned to groups. The first important lesson, then, is that some assumptions of statistical models, such as normality of errors, are relatively easy to check while others are more difficult or even impossible to check, as a result of which they may have to be accepted on rejected on the basis of knowledge of the content area.

The methods discussed in this chapter arose from three different lines of research. Each has advantages and disadvantages, but all have in common the modeling of selection into treatment groups. The first approach is the *econometric approach,* the second uses what are called *propensity scores,* and the third is called the *relative assignment* or *weighted adaptive regression approach.* The approaches differ in several respects, including how selection into groups is modeled and whether a specific form of the distribution of errors is assumed. These differences can be used to decide which method is more appropriate in a particular study or to test some assumptions of the approaches.

Econometric Approaches to the Modeling of Selection

Econometricians have contributed a great deal to the development of methods of modeling the selection process. This should not be surprising, since some of the most extensive and expensive evaluations—studies of the effects of a negative income tax—were conducted in the area of economics.

I will describe one of the simplest approaches of this type, both for pedagogical clarity and because this description should enable the researcher with access to common statistical packages to apply this approach. There are other ways of expressing the same model; in addition, there are different ways of estimating the parameters of each model (for example, least squares and maximum likelihood are the most common estimation methods).

The primary effect of using maximum likelihood rather than least squares in any type of statistical model is that maximum likelihood requires the specification of the underlying distribution (usually normal) in order to get estimates of the parameters of the model, while least squares generally requires such assumptions only for the hypothesis tests that follow the estimation. By using maximum likelihood, one gains the ability to make certain kinds of statistical hypothesis tests, although one loses flexibility because the form of the error distribution must be specified exactly. This is typical of the types of trade-offs that must generally be made in analyzing data from nonrandomized studies: by specifying the model more exactly, you are making more assumptions, but you gain in the ability to test hypotheses.

One form of the econometric model can be expressed in terms of two equations, one of which specifies the selection process, the other of which specifies the relationship between the outcome and the independent variables (covariates and treatment group dummy variable). If Y is the outcome variable, X and W are vectors of covariates where each variable in W is also in X, G is a dummy variable indicating group membership (usually $G = 0$ for the control group and $G = 1$ for the experimental group), and T is a variable on which selection is based, then the model is represented as

$$T = A\ X + e_1 \tag{1}$$
$$Y = B\ W + C\ G + e_2 \tag{2}$$

where A, B, and C are matrices of parameters and e_i are residuals for the two equations. If T is greater than 0 (or any arbitrary constant), then the participant is selected into the experimental group (that is, $G = 1$), and if T is less than or equal to zero, the participant is placed in the control group (that is, $G = 0$).

Unlike the regression discontinuity design, there is a residual in the equation for T, so that T is not directly observed. We know only that the variables in X are related to T and thus to the selection process. The presence of the residual term in equation 1 means that there may be factors other than those in X related to the selection process as well as pure random error.

Let us consider the statistical assumptions that are made in the specification of this model and how they translate into practical terms. There is NOT an assumption that the residual terms in the two equations are uncorrelated. If they were, then no special techniques would be needed; equation 2 would be sufficient by itself, and multiple regression would give an unbiased estimate of the effect of treatment.

As with the regression discontinuity design, there is an assumption that the model specified in equation 2 is correct, that is, that the linear model correctly describes the relationships and that if there are any interactions (including interactions with treatment condition) they are included in W. But, perhaps the most important assumption is one that seldom receives much attention: The residual terms must be unrelated to the covariates. In particular, if any variable is omitted from the selection equation that, if added, would predict T better and that, given W, affects the outcome, then there may be bias in the estimate of treatment effects (the parameter in C). The meaning of this assumption will become clear after we consider the other approaches.

Conceptually, the estimation process can be thought of as occurring in two steps, although this is not always true in practice. First, actual group membership is used as the dependent variable, and the variables in X are used to predict group membership. In some approaches, a simple linear model is used, which is equivalent to multiple regression of group membership on the variables in X if there are two groups and to discriminant analysis if there are more than two groups. The equation that results from this first step is used to calculate predicted group membership scores. These scores can be thought of as the predicted probability that an individual is in a particular group, given his or her values of the variables in X.

Next, the outcome variable Y is regressed on the covariates W and predicted (not actual) group membership G. If the assumptions of the model are true, then the coefficient of the predicted group membership variable gives an unbiased estimate of the treatment effect.

The literature on the econometric approach is extensive. The best summary of recent work in the area is Maddala's (1983). Several of the most important papers in this area that are relevant to evaluation research have been collected by Stromsdorfer and Farkas (1980). These papers include those by Heckman (1979) and Barnow and others (1980). One of the best elements of the Stromsdorfer and Farkas volume is the excellent introductions by the editors to the section on methodology and to individual papers. These introductory sections can give the reader a good overview of the area. An important new work that compares the assumptions needed in a wide variety of models is Heckman and Robb (1985).

The Propensity Score Approach

In the propensity score approach, the propensity (that is, the probability) of each person to be in the experimental rather than in the control group is estimated on the basis of a set of covariates that are thought to be related to group membership. The propensity score, rather than actual group membership, is then used in the statistical model for prediction of outcome. This gives an unbiased estimate of the treatment effect if, for any value on the covariates, the treatment group to which a person was assigned is not related to that person's outcome score. If this condition holds, then assignment to groups is said to be strongly ignorable. This is similar to the assumption in the econometric model that the residuals have zero mean and that they are uncorrelated with the predictors.

Both the conceptualization and the implementation of this method differ, at least in principle, from the other two methods. Each person is conceived of as having a pair of response scores, one of which would occur if the subject received the experimental treatment, the other if he or she received the control treatment. Thus, a subject can be characterized by the pair of numbers, such as (10,15), representing the scores that he or she would receive in the control and experimental conditions, respectively. However, each subject is observed in only one of the two conditions; only the response in that condition is observed, while the other is missing. This approach shows that nonrandomized studies have much in common with studies containing missing data.

To see how the critical assumption of strongly ignorable treatment assignment is expressed in this approach, consider a group of people who all have the same values on the covariates in the prediction equation (*W* in the econometric approach). For simplicity, suppose that there are two kinds of such people: those whose response vectors are (5,10) and those whose response vectors are (10,15). Each kind of person would score five points higher in the experimental treatment than in the control treatment, so the true causal effect is a five-point increase in the response variable.

If these people (all of whom have the same values on covariates in *W*) were randomly assigned to groups or if the variable used to assign them to groups was not related to their response vector, then there would be no bias in the estimate of treatment effects. For example, if blue-eyed people were assigned to the control group and brown-eyed people were assigned to the treatment group, then there would be no bias if eye color were unrelated to outcome, controlling for *W*. But, if scores on an IQ test were used to assign people to groups at each level of *W*, then there would probably be bias if the outcome was a test of cognitive ability. For example, if (at each level of *W*) the (5,10) people (low IQ) tended to get into the experimental group, where their observed scores are 10 while the (10,15) people (high IQ) tended to get into the control group where their observed scores are also 10, then the estimate of treatment effect would tend toward zero instead of five. In this case, IQ would increase the ability to classify people correctly into groups and IQ would be a determiner of the response, even when *W* is controlled.

Notice the difference between this situation and the situation in which IQ is related to the response and to treatment group overall (that is, ignoring *W*). In this description, the relationship between IQ and group is not conditional on values of *W*. This relationship, not the one we want, is the one we are able to observe. A simple (unconditional) relationship between an omitted variable and treatment group is not sufficient to cause bias; controlling for *W* may correct for the potential bias. We must depend on our knowledge of the content area about what variables we might have omitted from our study, and of course we may be wrong. This is why detecting such omissions can be difficult.

The estimation of the propensity score can be done in many ways. Some methods, such as logistic regression and probit models, are parametric approaches. These approaches are based on the specification of a particular form of relationship between group membership and the variable(s) determining group membership. Other methods use matching techniques to group together subjects who are similar on the predictors of treatment condition. Combinations of these methods can also be used, such as when the parametric model is used to estimate propensity scores, which are then used as a basis for the matching of subjects.

One minor difference between this method and similar methods is the assumption that, for all subjects, the probability of being in any group is nonzero. Strictly speaking, this assumption prevents the application of these techniques in situations such as the regression-discontinuity design. Nevertheless, the advantage is that the technique can be used when there is no continuous relationship between the covariates and assignment to treatment conditions. For example, if the variable used for assignment to treatment groups were categorical, such as the classroom in which a child was placed, then such techniques as the econometric methods are not applicable. But, if the probability of assignment to each group is neither zero nor one for each classroom, then the propensity score approach is applicable.

The propensity score approach has been developed by Donald B. Rubin and his colleagues. Holland and Rubin (1983) provide an excellent nontechnical introduction to Rubin's approach to causal inference. Rosenbaum and Rubin (1983a) is an important but more technical work. Rosenbaum (1984) and Rosenbaum and Rubin (1983b) discuss some approaches to the testing of assumptions and to the determination of sensitivity to violations of assumptions. The sources just enumerated contain references that can guide the reader who is interested in pursuing these techniques further.

The Relative Assignment Variable Approach

Like the propensity score approach, the relative assignment variable approach involves estimating for each person the probability of being in the treatment or the control group and then using that estimate instead of the actual dummy variable representing group membership in a regression equation predicting outcome. The main difference is that in this method no specific model of the relationship between the outcome variable Y and the assignment variable X is postulated; instead, a continuous function relating X to probability of assignment to the treatment group is assumed. The predicted probabilities are calculated by looking at each point on X (or a set of intervals covering the range of X) and finding the proportion of people in the experimental group.

The relative assignment variable approach thus uses what might be termed a model-free approach in order to estimate the probability of being in the experimental group, given a score on X. While the logistic regression approach and other related approaches, such as the probit, specify the nature of the relationship between X and probability of being in the experimental group, the relative assignment approach can handle nonlinear relationship, and the specific form of the relationship does not need to be known.

Variations in the relative assignment variable approach arise from the different ways of estimating the probability of being in the experimental group for each X value. Since X is assumed in principle to be a continuous variable, there are often very few people at each X value. This makes the calculation of probabilities very unreliable, so various strategies are used to base the calculation of probabilities on larger groups.

One approach is to divide the X variable into discrete categories. The divisions must satisfy two contradictory requirements: First, they must be wide, so that a large number of people are in each division; this will produce stable estimated probabilities. Second, they must at the same time be narrow, so that everyone in an interval has approximately the same probability of being in the experimental group. If the intervals are too wide, there may be too much variation in these probabilities for different people in the interval.

One way of creating these intervals is to divide X into increments of equal size. Another way of creating the intervals is to divide the X axis to that approximately the same number of people is in each interval. In either case, the number of intervals that are created (and thus the number of people in each interval) must be carefully chosen to try to address the problems discussed earlier.

Another way of calculating the predicted probabilities uses a technique common in time series analysis, the moving average. For each point on X, all people who are "close" to this point (in a sense well defined in each implementation of the method) are used as a group to calculate the probability of being in the experimental group. Unlike the processes described in the previous paragraph or the processes used in the propensity score method, where there is no overlap in the intervals created, there is almost complete overlap of adjacent intervals.

The techniques developed so far in this approach assume that there is only one covariate, X, which is used to determine assignment to treatment groups. In principle, these methods could be extended to handle multiple covariates. If covariates were categorical, then estimates of the probability of being in the experimental group could be made in each subgroup; that would make this approach equivalent to one version of the propensity score approach. Regardless of the form of the covariates, the probability of being in the experimental group could be calculated for each person by considering the observed proportion of people "like" that person who were in the experimental group, where "like" is defined in terms of the covariates. For example, one could define similarity between people in terms of the generalized Euclidean distance between them on the covariates; that is, people would be similar to the extent that they had similar values on the covariates. This technique would be comparable to the moving average technique used with one covariate.

A nontechnical presentation of the relative assignment variable approach can be found in Trochim (1984). Spiegelman (1979) and Trochim and Spiegelman (1980) are other useful publications.

Discussion

All three techniques assume that they have captured the treatment assignment process as well as possible. If it is possible to improve the prediction of treatment assignment, then there can be bias in the estimates of treatment effects. One simple check is to note whether all predicted probabilities are close either to zero or to one. If they are (and they correspond to the actual treatment groups!), then there is no room for improvement in the prediction of group membership and no possible problem with omitted variables.

Of course, these methods can be appropriate even when treatment assignment is not perfectly predictable. But, even if these assumptions are met, they will not work well under certain conditions. For example, if most or all probabilities predicted using logistic regression, probit, or related techniques are in the range of about .25 to about .75, then the relationship between the X variables and the probability of being in the treatment group is approximately linear. This creates estimation problems for some of the econometric methods. For all methods, the probabilities must show some variability. For example, all methods will fail if used to estimate treatment effects in a randomized study, where all probabilities are close to .50.

In order to check for such problems, analysts should always examine a histogram of the predicted probabilities of group membership. In addition, if there is a continuous covariate and the econometric approach has been used, then a plot of predicted probabilities against the covariate should be examined. It must be nonlinear in order for the estimation procedure to give useful results if the same covariates have been used in the selection equation and in the equation estimating treatment effects.

A troubling problem arises when one tries to decide when to use selection modeling techniques and when to use such techniques as structural equation models (see Chapter 6). Under some conditions, each technique gives unbiased estimates of treatment effects. Nevertheless, when one technique is appropriate, the other will usually give biased estimates of treatment effects. All that is known is that, if certain assumptions hold, then a particular method will give unbiased estimates. But, as we have seen, it is often difficult or impossible to determine whether the assumptions of these methods are true.

Several strategies are possible, none of which is perfect. Most involve trying alternative methods of analysis, each of which has different assumptions. This strategy will at least give an indication of the range of possible treatment effect sizes. At best, all estimates of the size of the treatment effect will be in a narrow range, showing that the estimate is not sensitive to differences in assumptions among the methods used.

The strategies that can be used include comparisons between selection modeling approaches and other approaches, comparisons among the various types of selection modeling approaches, and comparisons within types when there are different ways of implementing an approach. Some of these comparisons would be between qualitatively different models. Other sensitivity analyses could make comparisons within a model, where the assumed quantitative value of a parameter was successively fixed at different values. For example, in the econometric method, one could vary the correlation between the errors in the two equations and note how the bias in treatment effect estimates changed. These suggestions are at present more practical for research than for everyday use, because a complete set of analyses of a data set could be very time consuming.

In many cases, knowledge of subject matter will play a large role in determining whether to try selection modeling methods. If there is reason to believe that most of the variables that have determined selection into groups are known and that they have been measured, then selection modeling approaches are likely to work well. It is much easier to determine whether the statistical assumptions, such as normality, have been satisfied than it is to determine whether the overall approach is valid in a particular case. Some empirical evidence can be used, as indicated before: If predicted and actual group membership agree closely, selection modeling methods are justified.

Computer Programs

Only one widely available computer program can currently do the analyses discussed here. LIMDEP, by William Greene (1983, 1985), will perform most of the common econometric analyses. It is available for mainframe computers and for the IBM PC. The program is generally easy to use, although the manual may seem obscure in places due to the use of terminology and examples from economics. The program handles other problems that have similarities to those discussed here: attrition bias due to differential dropout from the groups studied and selection based on outcome variables. Other computer programs have been developed by individuals for their research; these programs may not be available generally.

Commonly available statistical packages can be used for some analyses. For example, one can use logistic regression (in BMDP or SPSS-X) or a probit model (in SAS) to model the selection process, calculate a variable with the predicted group from the results, and then use multiple regression for the final step. This two-step procedure has drawbacks—you cannot use the statistical tests from the final regression step to test for a treatment effect— but it also has advantages: Everyone can do it, and it makes fewer assumptions than maximum likelihood methods.

A FORTRAN program is available from William Trochim to do the moving average procedure described in the section on the relative assignment variable approach. As with the procedure mentioned in the previous paragraph, the output (relative assignment variable scores for each person) would then be used in a standard regression package.

Another way of proceeding is to write your own program. This is considerably more difficult, but it is possible, given the wide availability of functions (such as ZXMIN in IMSL) to find the minimum of any given function and the wide literature on econometric models, which contains the information that the researcher needs in order to specify the function to minimize and in order to calculate standard errors so that hypothesis tests can be made. LIMDEP has made it easy to do this for the more common models. If you need a more complex model, you will probably have to write your own program.

References

Barnow, B. S., Cain, G. G., and Goldberger, A. S. "Issues in the Analysis of Selectivity Bias." In E. W. Stromsdorfer and G. Farkas (eds.), *Evaluation Studies Review Annual.* Vol. 5. Beverly Hills, Calif.: Sage, 1980.

Greene, W. H. "LIMDEP: A Program for Estimating the Parameters of Qualitative and Limited-Dependent Variable Models." *American Statistician,* 1983, *37,* 170.

Greene, W. H. "LIMDEP: An Econometric Modeling Program for the IBM PC." *American Statistician,* 1985, *39,* 210.

Heckman, J. J. "Sample Selection Bias as a Specification Error." *Econometrics,* 1979, *47* (1), 153–161.

Heckman, J., and Robb, R. "Alternative Methods for Evaluating the Impact of Interventions." In J. Heckman and B. Singer (eds.), *Longitudinal Analysis of Labor Market Data.* New York: Cambridge University Press, 1985.

Holland, P. W., and Rubin, D. B. "On Lord's Paradox." In H. Wainer and S. Messick (eds.), *Principals [sic] of Modern Psychological Measurement: Festschrift for Frederic M. Lord.* Hillsdale, N.J.: Erlbaum, 1983.

Maddala, G. S. *Limited-Dependent and Qualitative Variables in Econometrics.* Cambridge, England: Cambridge University Press, 1983.

Rosenbaum, P. R. "From Association to Causation in Observational Studies: The Role of Tests of Strongly Ignorable Treatment Assignment." *Journal of the American Statistical Association,* 1984, *79,* 41–48.

Rosenbaum, P. R., and Rubin, D. B. "The Central Role of the Propensity Score in Observational Studies for Causal Effects." *Biometrika,* 1983a, *70,* 41–55.

Rosenbaum, P. R., and Rubin, D. B. "Assessing Sensitivity to an Unobserved Binary Covariate in an Observational Study with Binary Outcome." *Journal of the Royal Statistical Society, Series B,* 1983b, *45,* 212–218.

Spiegelman, C. H. "Estimating the Effect of a Large-Scale Pretest-Posttest Social Program." *Proceedings of the Social Statistics Section, American Statistical Association,* 1979, 370–373.

Stromsdorfer, E. W., and Farkas, G. (eds.). *Evaluation Studies Review Annual.* Vol. 5. Beverly Hills, Calif.: Sage, 1980.

Trochim, W. M. K. *Research Design for Program Evaluation: The Regression-Discontinuity Approach.* Beverly Hills, Calif.: Sage, 1984.

Trochim, W., and Spiegelman, C. H. "The Relative Assignment Variable Approach to Selection Bias in Pretest-Posttest Group Designs." *Proceedings of the Social Statistics Section, American Statistical Association,* 1980, 376–381.

David Rindskopf is associate professor in the educational psychology and psychology programs at the City University of New York Graduate Center. His primary areas of research are the theory and application of latent variable models, the design and analysis of nonrandomized studies, and the analysis of qualitative data.

Causal models often omit variables that should be included, use
variables that are measured fallibly, and ignore time lags. Such practices
can lead to severely biased estimates of effects. The discussion explains
these biases and shows how to take them into account.

Satisfying the Constraints of Causal Modeling

Charles S. Reichardt, Harry F. Gollob

Causal modeling can be used to estimate the size of effects when treatment conditions have not been assigned at random. For example, because participation in Head Start was not assigned at random, Magidson (1977; Magidson and Sörbom, 1982) used causal modeling to estimate the size of the program's effects on reading readiness. Similarly, because attendance at public and private schools was not assigned at random, Coleman, Hoffer, and Kilgore (1981) and Page and Keith (1981; Keith and Page, 1985) used causal modeling to estimate the differential effects of public and private schools on high school students' achievement.

Using nontechnical language, we describe how causal modeling operates. We also describe three sources of bias that can arise in causal modeling. It is unlikely that these sources of bias can be avoided or removed completely. Rather, the best that a researcher can do is to limit the size of the bias within a range. We introduce means of calculating appropriate ranges. In most cases of interest to social and behavioral scientists, the ranges that can

Work on this article was partially supported by NIMH Grant No. MH38305. We thank Melvin M. Mark and William M. K. Trochim for their helpful comments. Requests for reprints should be addressed to Charles S. Reichardt, Department of Psychology, University of Denver, Denver, Colorado 80208.

W. M. K. Trochim (ed.). *Advances in Quasi-Experimental Design and Analysis.*
New Directions for Program Evaluation, no. 31. San Francisco: Jossey-Bass, Fall 1986.

91

be set on the size of biases will be very large. This means that a great deal of uncertainty usually will surround the results of causal modeling. Both producers and consumers of research need to be aware of this uncertainty.

Causal Structures

Suppose that changes made in variables $X_1, X_2, \ldots,$ and X_K would cause changes in variable Y. In particular, suppose that a change in X_1 of one unit would cause a change in Y of B_1 units if $X_2, X_3, \ldots,$ and X_K were held constant. Similarly, suppose that a change in X_2 of one unit would cause a change in Y of B_2 units if $X_1, X_3, \ldots, X_K$ were held constant, and so on.

Further, suppose that the effects of changes in the X variables are additive. That is, suppose that a change of one unit in both X_1 and X_2 would cause a change in Y of $B_1 + B_2$ units if the other X's were held constant, that a change of one unit in each of $X_1, X_2,$ and X_3 would cause a change in Y of $B_1 + B_2 + B_3$ units if the other X's were held constant, and so on.

Finally, let E represent the aggregate effect of all the remaining causes of Y after holding constant all of the X variables. Then changes in Y are caused according to the following structure:

$$Y = B_1 X_1 + B_2 X_2 + \ldots + B_K X_K + E \tag{1}$$

For simplicity, but without loss of generality, all variables in this equation and elsewhere in the chapter are assumed to have been scaled to have a mean of zero.

Equation 1 will be called the causal structure of Y. The E variable is the causal residual and the Bs are the sizes of the causal effects.

Researchers often wish to know the values of the Bs in the causal structures of one or more variables. To estimate these values, researchers often use causal modeling techniques.

Causal Models

A structural equation model contains one or more equations. Each of the equations in a structural model sets a variable equal to a weighted additive combination of one or more other variables, plus a residual. For example, the variable Y can be set equal to a weighted additive combination of the variables $X_1, X_2, \ldots, X_K,$ plus a residual e. In this case, the structural equation would be

$$Y = b_1 X_1 + b_2 X_2 + \ldots + b_K X_K + e \tag{2}$$

where the b's are the weights.

Given data on Y and the X's, a structural equation model containing equation 2 could be fit so as to derive values for the b's. These fitted b's then could be used as estimates of the causal B's in the structure in equation 1. This use of structural equation modeling to estimate the size of causal effects is called *causal modeling*.

Because the model being fit to the data (equation 2) is so similar to the causal structure that underlies the data (equation 1), it may seem that the values derived for the b's must necessarily be unbiased estimates of the causal B's. Unfortunately, this is not so. Understanding the sources of bias requires understanding how values for the b's are chosen when the structural equation model containing equation 2 is fit to data.

Bias

When a model containing equation 2 is fit to data, the values chosen for the b's determine the values of the residual e. Choosing different values for the b's would result in different values for the fitted residual e. Structural equation modeling techniques choose values for the fitted b's in equation 2 so that the correlations between the fitted residual variable e and each of the X variables in the equation are as close to zero as possible. This is one of the fundamental constraints of causal modeling. The constraints under which causal modeling operates are more complex than given here. A more complete and rigorous explication of the constraints would greatly complicate the discussion but would not change the implications that follow.

In contrast, in the causal structure in equation 1 the causal residual E and the X variables do not need to be related in any particular way. Whether the b's derived from the fitted model are unbiased estimates of the B's in the causal structure depends on the relationship between the causal residual E and the X's in the causal structure in equation 1.

If the causal residual E in equation 1 is uncorrelated with the X's, the b's derived from fitting equation 2 will be unbiased estimates of the causal B's. Intuitively, the reason is the following: By choosing the b's so that the fitted e in equation 2 is uncorrelated with the X's, structural equation modeling is mirroring how the causal E in equation 1 is related to the X's, and as a result the fitted b's will mirror the causal B's.

On the other hand, if the causal residual E in equation 1 is correlated with one or more of the X's, the b's derived from fitting equation 2 generally will be biased estimates of the causal B's. This is because choosing the b's so that the fitted e is uncorrelated with the X's in equation 2 means that structural equation modeling doesn't mirror the way in which the causal E is correlated with one or more of the X's in equation 1, and so the b's will not mirror the causal B's.

Figure 1 uses data and a causal structure for three hypothetical groups of individuals to illustrate the presence and absence of bias. Each group is described in a different panel of the figure. In each panel, changes in X cause changes in Y in accordance with the simple causal structure

$$Y = BX + E \tag{3}$$

The solid line in each panel has slope B which shows the size of the change in Y caused by a unit increase in X. The dots in the three panels show how the data on X and Y in each group are scattered around these lines. Most of the dots do not fall exactly on the lines because of the other influences besides X that are operating on Y. The vertical distance from the solid lines to each dot is the value of E for each individual, which is the aggregate effect of these other influences. The E's were chosen so that the correlation between X and the E's is different in each panel. As a result, the pattern of dots is different in each panel.

The E's in panel A are uncorrelated with the values of X. This means that large values of X are just as often associated with positive values of E as with negative values of E. Similarly, small values of X are just as often associated with positive values of E as with negative values of E. In contrast, the E's in panel B are positively correlated with the values of X. This is because positive values of E usually occur with large values of X while negative values of E usually occur with small values of X. Finally, the E's in panel C are negatively correlated with X.

Now consider the use of structural equation techniques to fit the following model to each of the three data sets:
$$Y = bX + e. \tag{4}$$
The value of b derived by making e uncorrelated with X as is done by fitting equation 4 using structural equation modeling is given by the slope of the dashed line in each panel. The values of e are the vertical distances between the dashed lines and the data points.

In panel A, the dashed line coincides with the solid line, indicating that the value of b chosen by structural equation modeling is an unbiased estimate of the causal B. Structural equation modeling produces an unbiased estimate because making the fitted e uncorrelated with X mirrors the way the causal E is uncorrelated with X.

In contrast, the dashed lines do not coincide with the solid lines in panels B and C. This means that for these two groups the values of the b's chosen by structural equation modeling are biased estimates of the causal B. The biases arise because the fitted e's are made to be uncorrelated with X while the causal E's are correlated with X. Because the causal E is positively correlated with X in panel B, the fitted b is larger than the causal B. Conversely, because the causal E is negatively correlated with X in panel C, the fitted b is less than the causal B. Indeed, in panel C the fitted b is negative while the causal B is positive. It also is possible for the fitted b to be positive while the causal B is negative.

Figure 1 reveals the bias when there is only one X variable in the structural equation model. The biases that arise when more than one X variable is present are usually more complex. With only one X variable, a causal E that is positively correlated with X results in a positive bias in the fitted b, while a causal E that is negatively correlated with X results in a negative bias in the fitted b. With more than one X variable in the model, the direction of bias depends on how the causal E is related to all the X's in the model

Figure 1. Three Hypothetical Populations Where *X* Has the Same Effect
on *Y* but the Aggregate Effects of Omitted Variables Differ

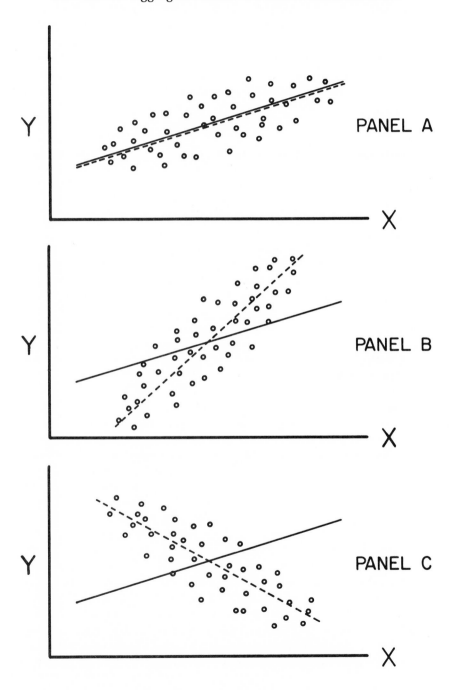

and on how the X's are interrelated. Even if E is correlated with only one of the X variables in the model, the b's for all the X's can be biased if the X's are intercorrelated.

There are many reasons why the causal E in equation 1 might be correlated with one or more of the X variables so that the b's derived from use of structural equation modeling to fit equation 2 would be biased estimates of the B's. Three prominent sources of bias and means for taking them into account are described in the sections that follow.

Omitted Variables

In the causal structure of equation 1, the residual E is the aggregate effect of all the variables besides the X's that influence Y. Because the variables that make up E are not specified separately in the model like the X variables, they are called *omitted variables*.

Biases Due to Omitted Variables. If all the variables that are omitted from a causal structure and therefore that make up E are uncorrelated with all the X variables that are included in the equation, then necessarily E will be uncorrelated with all the X variables. However, if any omitted variable is correlated with one or more of the X variables, E can be correlated with one or more of the X variables. In this way, omitting a variable that influences Y and that is correlated with one or more of the X variables included in the model can bias the estimates of effects derived using structural equation techniques.

For example, Scarr (1985) found that the omission of background variables, such as mother's vocabulary, altered estimates of the effect of mother's positive discipline on a child's communication skills. Specifically, the estimate from a model that included mother's vocabulary was a statistically nonsignificant 0.11, while the estimate from a model that omitted mother's vocabulary was twice as large and statistically significant. If the estimate derived from a model that included mother's vocabularly is unbiased, the estimate derived from the model that omitted mother's vocabulary is biased. The reason for the bias is that mother's vocabulary (the omitted variable) influences child's communication skills (the Y variable) and is correlated with mother's positive discipline (which is an X variable in the model).

In the preceding example, omitting a variable from the model increased the size of an effect estimate. Specifically, omitting a background variable made mother's positive discipline look more effective than it would have appeared if the background variable had been included. Instead of increasing the size of an effect estimate, omitting a variable also can decrease an effect estimate. For example, Magidson (1977) uses intellectual background in his structural equation model to assess the effect of Head Start. Because intellectual background was negatively correlated with enrollment in the Head Start program (that is, the children who received the program were those who tended to need it the most), if he had omitted the background variable the estimate of the effect of Head Start would have been shifted negatively and therefore would have made the program look harmful.

It is generally not possible to include all the causes of a dependent variable in a causal model. Further, when treatment conditions are not assigned at random, it is likely that many of the causal variables that are omitted are correlated with variables that are included. For this reason, it is unlikely that biases due to omitted variables can be avoided in quasi-experimental designs.

Taking Account of Omitted Variables. The bias due to omitted variables is a function of the correlations between E and the included X variables. In turn, these correlations are a function of the variances and covariances of E and the included X variables. If these variances and covariances were known exactly, the size of the bias could be calculated exactly and therefore removed. Unfortunately, it is unlikely that these variances and covariances can be known exactly. Rather, the best that can be done is to estimate the variances and covariances within ranges and thereby limit the bias within a range.

In an effort to establish bounds on the size of the bias due to an omitted variable, Reichardt and Gollob (1986) have shown that the largest and smallest bias in b_j occurs when an omitted variable is correlated with X_j but uncorrelated with the other X variables in the model. Based on this result and using data on the X variables in the model, Reichardt and Gollob (1986) show how the size of the bias can be bounded if an upper limit on the variance of E can be specified. Letting σ_E represent the standard deviation of E, if σ_E is known to be no greater than σ^+_E, the size of the bias in b_j as an estimate of B_j must fall in the range

$$\pm \frac{\sigma^+_E}{\sigma_X \sqrt{1 - R_X^2}} \tag{5}$$

where σ_X is the standard deviation of X_j and R_X^2 is the squared multiple correlation of X_j with the other X's included in the model. The values of σ_X and R_X^2 are given by the data. However, an upper limit on σ_E isn't given by the data. It must be set by relying on knowledge of the characteristics of the causes of Y that have been omitted from the model. For example, if E were known to be correlated positively with each of the included variables, it can be shown that the variance of E cannot be greater than the variance of Y. Although it may be difficult to obtain the substantive knowledge needed to set an upper limit on σ_E, such a limit is necessary if a bound on the size of the bias is to be established, whether by the formula given here or by any other means.

Narrower bounds than those in equation 5 can be established given additional knowledge. For example, if substantive knowledge enabled one to set an upper limit on the multiple correlation of E with the X's, the bounds on the bias in equation 5 can be reduced by a factor of that upper limit. Thus, the smaller the multiple correlation of E with the X's, the narrower the limit on the bias. Reichardt and Gollob (1986) show how to narrow the bounds on the bias given knowledge about other quantities as well.

Bounds on the bias also can be narrowed through the design of a study. For example, bounds on the bias can be narrowed by including X variables in the model so as to leave as little variance in E as possible and to minimize the correlation between whatever E remains and the included X's. Bounds also tend to be narrow to the extent that the X variables included in the model are uncorrelated with each other. Unfortunately, adding X variables so as to reduce the variance in E often tends to increase the amount of intercorrelation that exists among the X's and vice versa.

An Example of Setting Bounds. Keith and Page (1985) used causal modeling to compare the effect of Catholic high schools on the achievement of black students with the effect of public high schools on such students. Their model regressed a measure of achievement on measures of school type (that is, Catholic or public), family background, and ability. Using variables standardized to have unit variance, Catholic schools were estimated to have an average effect of 0.14 on achievement above and beyond the effect of public schools.

Other researchers have used causal models to estimate the size of the effects of educational programs without including a measure of ability. For example, Magidson (1977; Magidson and Sörbom, 1982) estimated the effect of Head Start by regressing a measure of achievement on measures of Head Start participation and family background but not of ability. Similarly, Coleman and others (1981) compared the effect of private high schools with the effect of public high schools by regressing a measure of achievement on measures of school type and family background but not of ability. If one thought that a better causal model would be obtained by including a measure of ability, one would want to know how much difference resulted from the omission of ability. The data from Keith and Page (1985) are used below to illustrate how bounds can be set on the size of the bias due to the omission of ability.

If Keith and Page (1985) had omitted ability from their causal model, the estimate of the differential effects of Catholic and public schools would have been 0.28 rather than 0.14. Assuming that data on ability were not available, a researcher would know neither the exact size of this bias nor exactly how ability was related to the variables that were included in the analysis. But, using knowledge of the size of parameters in other populations where ability had been measured, a researcher might be able to set reasonable limits on the size of the parameters in the population at hand. Using results more elaborate than in equation 5, Reichardt and Gollob (1986) show that if a researcher could set limits on unknown parameters within plus or minus 0.2 of the true values for standardized variables, the size of the resulting bias would be bounded between −0.06 and 0.42. This means that the effect of school type would be estimated to lie between −0.14 (that is, 0.28 minus 0.42) and 0.34 (that is, 0.28 minus 0.06), which indeed contains the actual value of 0.14.

If narrower limits could be set on the size of the unknown parameters, narrower bounds could be set on the size of the bias. For example, if limits could be set on parameters that were within plus or minus 0.1 of the true values for standardized variables, the effect of school type would be estimated to lie between 0.02 and 0.24 rather than between −0.14 and 0.34 as just shown.

In most applications of causal modeling it is unlikely that limits on the unknown parameters can be set that are within 0.1 of the true values, and it is sometimes even unlikely that limits can be set within 0.2. For this reason, the bounds that can be set on the size of the bias due to omitted variables often will be large. Although this result may be unpleasant, it is an accurate reflection of the uncertainty that often surrounds the results of causal modeling in the social sciences.

Imperfect Measurement

Measures of variables often contain error. For example, achievement tests do not perfectly measure achievement, because test scores are influenced by additional factors, such as motivation and alertness. Even measures that are perfectly reliable can contain error. For example, a researcher unable to measure physical maturity might use age as a proxy. Nevertheless, while age can be measured with great reliability, it contains substantial error as a measure of physical maturity, because individuals mature at different rates.

Biases Due to Imperfect Measurement. Measurement error in the X variables in a model can bias estimates derived from structural equation modeling. The reason is that error can make the causal E correlated with the observed X's in the causal structure of equation 1. To see how measurement error can produce a correlation between E and the X variables, suppose that X influences Y in accordance with the simple causal structure

$$Y = B \, X + E \tag{6}$$

where E is uncorrelated with X. But, suppose that only a fallible measure of X is available, not X itself. Specifically, suppose that X^* is observed where

$$X^* = X + U \tag{7}$$

and U represents error. In general, because U is a part of X^*, U will be correlated with X^* (Berkson, 1950).

By rearranging equation 7, the true X score can be expressed as the fallible score X^* minus the error U. That is,

$$X = X^* - U. \tag{8}$$

Substituting equation 8 for X in equation 6 allows the causal structure for Y to be expressed in terms of the fallible score as

$$Y = B (X^* - U) + E \qquad (9)$$

which can be rearranged further to produce

$$Y = B X^* + (E - B U). \qquad (10)$$

Finally, this equation can be rewritten as

$$Y = B X^* + E^* \qquad (11)$$

where $E^* = (E - B U)$. This is the true causal structure written in terms of the fallible measure. Because U is a part of both E^* and X^*, in general E^* will be correlated with X^*. Thus, if the fallible variable X^* were fit in the model

$$Y = b X^* + e \qquad (12)$$

using structural equation techniques, b would be a biased estimate of B, because, in terms of the causal structure for the fallible variables (equation 11), the residual is correlated with an included variable. Also see Cochran (1968), Campbell and Erlebacher (1970), and Reichardt (1979).

If the measurement error in a variable is uncorrelated with the true score, the b for that variable is shifted closer to zero, while the b's for other variables in the model are shifted closer to what they would be if the fallible variable had been omitted from the model. For example, given a model regressing Y on both X_1 and X_2, random error in X_1 shifts b_1 toward zero and b_2 toward the value that it would have taken if X_1 had been omitted from the regression (Reichardt, 1979). However, if the error in an X variable is correlated with the true score, the values of the b's can be shifted in the opposite direction. Correlated errors can arise from many sources, including floor and ceiling effects.

The bias in the values of the b's due to errorful measurement can be substantial. For example, by taking account of error, Magidson (1977; Magidson and Sörbom, 1982) derived a positive estimate for the effect of Head Start, while the original analysis, which ignored the biasing effect of measurement error, had produced a negative estimate.

Similarly, Director (1979) found that biases due to errorful measurement could make manpower training programs look harmful. Specifically, Director (1979) found that biases were likely to have reduced the estimated effectiveness of manpower training programs in seven independent studies. This was because in each study it appeared that the experimental group was of lower ability than the control group; ability was fallibly measured; the measurement error was largely uncorrelated with the true score, so that the error produced a bias in the same direction as the bias caused by omitting the ability variable; and, given the initial differences between the groups, such an omission makes the program look less effective than it was. Director also found eleven independent studies in which a bias due to measurement error was likely to have increased the estimated effectiveness of the program. This was because the experimental group was of higher ability than the control group, although the other characteristics of these studies were the same as the studies that were likely to be biased in the opposite direction.

In the original analyses conducted for these studies, the biasing effects of measurement error were not taken into account. Interestingly, in six of the seven studies in which the bias would make the program look less effective than it was, the program was estimated to have a harmful effect, while in all eleven studies in which the bias would make the program look more effective than it was, the program was estimated to have a beneficial effect.

It is good practice to try to measure the variables to be included in a causal model as accurately as possible. However, most constructs can be measured only fallibly, no matter how sophisticated the measurement process is.

Taking Account of Imperfect Measurement. A number of procedures have been devised to remove the bias due to measurement error. One of the most popular procedures uses multiple measures of each construct and computer programs such as LISREL (Jöreskog and Sörbom, 1984) or EQS (Bentler, 1985) to triangulate on the true scores. Any such procedure requires that restrictions be imposed on the structure of the measurement error. For example, one common restriction is that the correlations between measurement errors and true scores must be fixed a priori at their true values. These values are not likely to be known exactly, so the analytical model is not likely to be perfectly correct. (For example, the correlations between errors and true scores are typically fixed at zero, although this can be far from the true value, because measurement error is often far from random.) Instead, the best that can be done is to specify the degree of correlation within a range and thereby limit the bias within a range.

The bias can be limited within a range using multiple analyses. For example, bounds can be set by running a series of LISREL analyses that impose a range of restrictions. Unfortunately, such a strategy usually requires a large number of analyses, because there are so many plausible restrictions and because the worst biases can arise when restrictions take on intermediate rather than extreme values. These difficulties can be avoided if bounds are set using the analytical results in Reichardt and Gollob (1986). Given a plausible range of restrictions on the structure of the measurement error, this approach allows bounds to be set both on the bias that arises in analyses that ignore measurement error and on the bias that remains in analyses that attempt to take measurement error into account but do so imperfectly.

Ignoring Time Lags

In causal modeling, researchers often use measures of causes that are taken at the same time as measures of presumed effects. For example, if Y is regressed on X so as to estimate the effect of X on Y, values of both X and Y are measured at time t. This situation is graphically represented in panel A of Figure 2, where subscripts indicate time of measurement and arrows indicate that Y_t is being modeled as a function of X_t and e. Causes and effects often are measured at the same time because a single survey instrument is used to measure all the variables in the model. For example, Duncan, Haller and Portes (1971) used measures collected on a single survey at a single point in time to estimate the effect of a friend's occupational aspiration on a teenager's own occupational aspiration.

Effects Take Time to Occur. Although cross-sectional models like the one depicted in panel A are often used, causes and effects do not operate as depicted in that figure. Rather than occuring at the same time, cause and effect are separated by a lag. For example, it takes time for aspirin to have an effect on headache pain, because it takes time for the aspirin to dissolve, to be absorbed into the bloodstream, and to travel to the brain. Of course, some very rapid effects appear to occur instantaneously. For example, it appears that pushing down on one end of a seesaw causes the other end to rise simultaneously. But in fact a very brief time lag is present. This is because the effect of pushing down on one end of the seesaw is transmitted to the other end at the speed of light rather than instantaneously. In all the examples we have come across in the social sciences, the presence of a time lag between cause and effect is indisputable and often is substantial.

Because effects take time to occur, it is panel B in Figure 2 rather than panel A that illustrates how causes produce effects (Gollob and Reichardt, 1985, in press; Reichardt and Gollob, 1984; Heise, 1975; James, Mulaik and Brett, 1982). The difference is that, rather than X at time t causing Y at time t, it is X at an earlier time, $t - 1$, that causes Y at time t. And, while this cause is operating, Y_{t-1} is influencing Y_t as well. (The curved double-headed arrow in panel B indicates that Y_{t-1} can be correlated with X_{t-1}. Such a correlation might arise because a previous X variable, say X_{t-2}, influenced both Y_{t-1} and X_{t-1}, just as X_{t-1} influences both Y_t and X_{t}.) For example, in the study by Duncan and others (1971), a change in the occupational aspiration of a teenager's friend would have taken time to influence the teenager's own level of aspiration. In addition, a teenager's occupational aspiration at time t would not only be influenced by a friend's occupational aspiration at time $t - 1$ but also by the teenager's own occupational aspiration at time $t - 1$.

By fitting the model in panel A rather than the model in panel B, Y_{t-1} is omitted. As previously shown, omitting a variable can cause bias in the estimates of effects. Further, by fitting the model in panel A rather than the model in panel B, X_t is included in place of X_{t-1}. When X changes over time, using X_t in place of X_{t-1} is mathematically equivalent to including X_{t-1} in the model but measuring it with error. As shown previously, measuring a variable with error can also cause bias in the estimates of effects.

The biases produced by ignoring time lags in this fashion can be

Figure 2. A Cross-Sectional Model and a Longitudinal Causal Structure

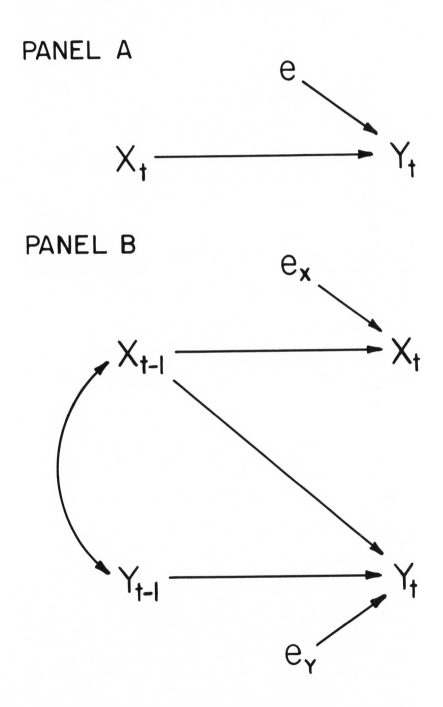

substantial. For example, Duncan and others (1971) estimated that the effect of a friend's occupational aspiration on a teenager's own occupational aspiration was 0.41 when time lags were ignored, while Reichardt and Gollob (1984) estimated that the effect would have been only 0.10 if time lags had been taken into account. Even if the time that elapses between cause and effect is very short, the bias can be large.

Taking Account of Time Lags. Typically, the best way to take account of time lags is to fit longitudinal models as in panel B rather than cross-sectional models as in panel A. Although retrospective accounts taken at time t can be used to obtain data for time $t - 1$, usually the best way to obtain longitudinal data is to measure variables directly both at time t and at time $t - 1$.

When data are available only for time t, Reichardt and Gollob (1984; Gollob and Reichardt, 1985, 1986, in press) still recommend that longitudinal models be employed, although this means using latent variables to represent data that are unavailable for time $t - 1$. Implementing such a "latent longitudinal" model requires knowledge of a number of variances and correlations among the observed and the unobserved variables. It is unlikely that the exact values of these variances and correlations will be known, so it is unlikely that time lags can be taken into account exactly. Rather, the best one can do is to estimate the required variances and correlations within a range and thereby take account of time lags within a range.

Time lags can be taken into account within a range by using multiple analyses. That is, bounds can be set on the bias by fitting the data with a series of latent longitudinal models, where each model fixes the unknown variances and correlations at different plausible values. Unfortunately, this strategy usually requires a great many computer runs, because there are so many plausible combinations of values for the variances and correlations, and because the worst biases can arise when the values of the variances and correlations are intermediate rather than extreme. Alternatively, bounds can be set using the analytical results in Reichardt and Gollob (1986). This approach allows bounds to be set both on the biases that arise in cross-sectional models because time lags are ignored and on any biases that remain in latent longitudinal models.

Model Fit

The sizes of the biases that have been described are not limited by how well a model fits the data. This is because no matter how well or how poorly a model fits the data, it can be wrong as a model of the true causal structure. For example, other things being equal, a large multiple correlation between Y and the X variables is preferred to a small one, but the value of the multiple correlation, by itself, doesn't limit the size of the bias. Even if the multiple correlation is unity, the bias can be any size from positive infinity to negative infinity.

Similarly, the size of the bias is not limited by the results of a chi-square goodness-of-fit test. The chi-square test and related indices (Bentler and Bonett, 1980) reveal how well a model reproduces the variances and covariances in the data, but the value of the chi-square, by itself, does not limit the size of the bias. Even when the chi-square is zero, which means that the reproduction is perfect, the bias can be very large.

Conclusions

Several sources of bias that are likely to arise in causal modeling have been described in this chapter. These biases can be substantial, and they seldom can be avoided completely. Rather, the most that a researcher can hope to do is to limit the biases within ranges. Reseachers should try to design their studies so that biases can be bounded within narrow ranges.

Often, in spite of one's best efforts, biases can be limited only within very large ranges, which means that the results of causal analysis are equivocal. The degree of equivocality that exists seldom is reported. Not to report the uncertainty can be misleading to policy makers and to other investigators, and ultimately it could undermine the credibility of evaluation research. It is desirable to be able to find answers that lie within narrow bounds, and there is much pressure on evaluators to do so. But, when one cannot, it is best to be forthright about the uncertainty that is present.

There are other ways of assessing the effects of social programs besides the methods that typically fall under the rubric of causal modeling. Alternatives includes analyses based on selection modeling (described by Rindskopf in Chapter Five of this volume), regression-discontinuity designs (Trochim, 1984), interrupted time-series designs (McCleary and Hay, 1980), and randomized experiments (Berk and others, 1985). Severe biases can arise with any of these approaches. Even randomized experiments are not immune. For example, Fetterman (1982) describes an evaluation whose outcome was probably affected more by the antagonism engendered by random assignment of individuals to treatments than by the treatment itself. Regardless of the research design and analysis strategy, bias seldom can be avoided completely; the most that can be accomplished is to limit the bias within a range. But, in many situations one can obtain a narrower range using methods other than causal modeling. For example, although they have weaknesses, randomized experiments make the expected correlation between the treatment and all background variables zero, and this often greatly reduces the sizes of biases due to omitting variables, measuring variables with error, and failing to take account of time lags. Because they often produce results that are less equivocal than the results produced with causal modeling, randomized

experiments and other approaches to estimating program effects deserve to
be considered either in addition to or in place of causal modeling.

References

Bentler, P. M. *Theory and Implementation of EQS: A Structural Equation Program.* Los
  Angeles: BMDP Statistical Software, 1985.
Bentler, P. M., and Bonnet, D. G. "Significance Tests and Goodness of Fit in the
  Analysis of Covariance Structures." *Psychological Bulletin,* 1980, *88,* 588–606.
Berk, R. A., Boruch, R. F., Chambers, D. L., Rossi, P. H., and White, A. D. "Social
  Policy Experimentation: A Position Paper." *Evaluation Review,* 1985, *9,* 387–429.
Berkson, J. "Are There Two Regressions?" *Journal of the American Statistical Association,*
  1950, *45,* 164–180.
Campbell, D. T., and Erlebacher, A. E. "How Regression Artifacts in Quasi-Experi-
  mental Evaluations Can Mistakenly Make Compensatory Education Look
  Harmful." In J. Hellmuth (ed.), *Compensatory Education: A National Debate.* Vol. 3.
  New York: Brunner/Mazel, 1970.
Cochran, W. G. "Errors of Measurement in Statistics." *Technometrics,* 1968, *10,* 637–
  666.
Coleman, J., Hoffer, T., and Kilgore, S. *Public and Private Schools.* Chicago: University of
  Chicago, 1981. (ED 197 503)
Director, S. M. "Underadjustment Bias in the Evaluation of Manpower Training."
  Evaluation Quarterly, 1979, *3,* 190–218.
Duncan, O. D., Haller, A. O., and Portes, A. "Peer Influences on Aspirations: A
  Reinterpretation." In H. M. Blalock, Jr. (ed.), *Causal Models in the Social Sciences.*
  Chicago: Aldine, 1971.
Fetterman, D. M. "Ibsen's Baths: Reactivity and Insensitivity." *Educational Evaluation
  and Policy Analysis,* 1982, *4,* 261–279.
Gollob, H. F., and Reichardt, C. S. "Building Time Lags into Causal Models of
  Cross-sectional Data." *Proceedings of the Social Statistics Section of the American Statistical
  Association.* Washington D.C.: American Statistical Association, 1985.
Gollob, H. F., and Reichardt, C. S. *The Latent Longitudinal Approach to Causal Modeling.*
  Denver, Colo.: University of Denver, Dept. of Psychology, 1986.
Gollob, H. F., and Reichardt, C. S. "Allowing for Time Lags in Causal Models." *Child
  Development,* in press.
Heise, D. R. *Causal Analysis.* New York: Wiley, 1975.
James, L. R., Mulaik, S. A., and Brett, J. M. *Causal Analysis: Assumptions, Models, and
  Data.* Beverly Hills, Calif: Sage, 1982.
Jöreskog, K. G., and Sörbom, D. *LISREL VI: Analysis of Linear Structural Relationships by
  the Method of Maximum Likelihood, Instrumental Variables, and Least Squares Methods. User's
  Guide.* Mooresville, Ind.: Scientific Software, 1984.
Keith, T. Z., and Page, E. B. "Do Catholic High Schools Improve Minority Student
  Achievement?" *American Educational Research Journal,* 1985, *22,* 337–349.
Magidson, J. "Toward a Causal Model Approach for Adjusting for Preexisting Dif-
  ferences in the Nonequivalent Control Group Situation: A General Alternative to
  ANCOVA." *Evaluation Quarterly,* 1977, *1,* 399–420.
Magidson, J., and Sörbom, D. "Adjusting for Confounding Factors in Quasi-Experi-
  ments: Another Reanalysis of the Westinghouse Head Start Evaluation." *Educa-
  tional Evaluation and Policy Analysis,* 1982, *4,* 321–329.
McCleary, R., and Hay, R. A. *Applied Time Series Analysis.* Beverly Hills, Calif.: Sage,
  1980.

Page, E. B., and Keith, T. Z. "Effects of U.S. Private Schools: A Technical Analysis of Two Recent Claims." *Educational Researcher,* 1981, *10,* 7–17.

Reichardt, C. S. "The Statistical Analysis of Data from Nonequivalent Group Designs." In T. D. Cook and D. T. Campbell (eds.), *Quasi-Experimentation: Design and Analysis Issues for Field Settings.* Chicago: Rand McNally, 1979.

Reichardt, C. S., and Gollob, H. F. *Structural Equation Models of Reciprocal Causality.* Denver, Colo.: University of Denver, Dept. of Psychology, 1984.

Reichardt, C. S., and Gollob, H. F. *Setting Limits on the Bias Due to Omitted Variables.* Denver, Colo.: University of Denver, Dept. of Psychology, 1986.

Scarr, S. "Constructing Psychology: Making Facts and Fables for our Time." *American Psychologist,* 1985, *40,* 499–512.

Trochim, W. M. K. *Research Design for Program Evaluation: The Regression-Discontinuity Approach.* Beverly Hills, Calif.: Sage, 1984.

Charles S. Reichardt is associate professor of psychology at the University of Denver. His research focuses on the logic and practice of estimating effects.

Harry F. Gollob is professor of psychology at the University of Denver. His research interests include the development of quantitative models of social judgment, dyadic interaction, and employment discrimination.

Index

A

Adler, E., 40–42, 45
Alexander, J. K., 38–41, 45
Ambron, S. R., 33, 44, 54, 61, 65

B

Barnow, B. S., 82, 88
Bassett, R., 58, 65
Becker, H. S., 71, 76
Bentler, P. M., 17, 25, 101, 105, 106
Berger, D. E., 22, 27, 53, 66
Berk, R. A., 37, 44, 105, 106
Berkson, J., 99, 106
Berman, J. S., 42, 44
Betsey, C. L., 10, 25
Bias: in experiments, 37, 42, 93–96; from imperfect measurement, 99–101; and model fit, 104–105; removing, 80–87. *See also* Causal modeling
Bickman, L., 3, 6
Blockage model. *See* Causal relationships
Bloom, H. S., 16, 25
Bonnet, D. G., 105, 106
Boruch, R. F., 2, 6, 10, 15, 25, 26, 106
Breitrose, P., 38, 39, 40, 41, 42, 45
Brett, J. M., 102, 106
Brown, B. W., 38–41, 45

C

Cacioppo, J. T., 58, 65
Cain, G. G., 82, 88
Campbell, D. T., 1–3, 6–7, 15, 19–21, 25–26, 29–30, 33, 35–39, 44, 47–49, 52–65, 67–69, 71, 73–74, 76–77, 100, 106
Cardiovascular education, study of, 38–42
Causal modeling: bias in, 93–96; model of, 93–93; omitted variables in, 96–99; structures of, 92; time lags in, 101–104
Causal relationships: blockage model of, 57; criteria for, 11; critical multiplism and, 32; Einhorn and Hogarth model of, 12–13; enhancement model and, 58; features of, 12–13; hypothesis of, 33–36; judgment of, 11–12, 14; pattern-matching model and, 58–59; purification model and, 58; study of, 57–59. *See also* Quasi-experimental analysis
Chadwick, R. W., 77
Chalmers, T. C., 10, 26
Chambers, D. L., 105, 106
Chen, H. T., 2, 3, 7, 16, 26, 33, 44
Cialdini, R. B., 58, 65
Cliff, N., 17, 26
Cochran, W. G., 100, 106
Coleman, J., 91, 99, 106
Coleman, J. S., 34, 44
Computer programs for selection modeling. *See* Selection modeling
Construct validity, 71
Cook, T. D., 1, 3–4, 7, 15, 19, 26, 29, 33–39, 44–45, 47, 49, 52–61, 63–65, 67–68, 71, 73, 77
Cooper, J., 57, 65
Cordray, D. S., 10, 22, 25–27, 53, 66
Crano, W. D., 21, 26
Critical multiplism: benefits of, 31, 33; multiple operationalism and, 30; origin of, 4, 29; quasi-experimentation and, 30–44; trade-offs of, 31
Cronbach, L. J., 2, 3, 5, 7, 33, 44, 47–50, 52, 53, 55–59, 63, 64, 65
Crosse, S., 9, 15, 27
Cues to causality, 12, 13, 14, 22
Curtin, T. R., 36, 44

D

D'Andrade, R., 69, 77
Director, S. M., 16, 21, 26, 100, 106
Distortion: differential and, 24; null hypothesis and, 24; redundancy and, 24
Dixon, M. C., 10, 27
Dornbush, S. M., 33, 44, 54, 61, 65